THE
ULTIMATE
TYRANNY

By Eugene J. McCarthy

Frontiers in American Democracy

The Crescent Dictionary of American Politics

A Liberal Answer to the Conservative Challenge

The Limits of Power: America's Role in the World

The Year of the People

The Hard Years: A Look at Contemporary America and American Institutions

America Revisited: 150 Years after Tocqueville

A Political Bestiary: Viable Alternatives, Impressive Mandates and Other Fables (with James J. Kilpatrick)

Poetry

Other Things and the Aardvark

Ground Fog and Night

For Children

Mr. Raccoon and His Friends

☆

THE ULTIMATE TYRANNY

The Majority over the Majority

☆

Eugene J. McCarthy

☆

Harcourt Brace Jovanovich
New York and London

Requests for permission to make copies of
any part of the work should be mailed to:
Permissions, Harcourt Brace Jovanovich, Inc.
757 Third Avenue, New York, N.Y. 10017

The letter of November 13, 1978, from
Stewart R. Mott to the Hon. Neil O. Staebler
is used by permission.

Printed in the United States of America

Library of Congress Cataloging in Publication Data

McCarthy, Eugene J 1916–
The ultimate tyranny.

Includes index.
1. United States—Constitutional history.
2. Liberty of speech—United States. 3. Assembly,
Right of—United States. 4. Administrative agencies—
United States. I. Title.
JK271.M242   342.73'029   79-3530
ISBN 0-15-192581-X

Set in Linotype Times Roman

First edition

B C D E

Contents

THE
ULTIMATE
TYRANNY

The Book, the Harp,
the Sword, and the Plow

Albert Schweitzer, speaking of the order of nature, said that if we lose our capacity to foresee and to forestall, we will end up destroying the earth.

In the order of politics, economics, and social organization, failure to foresee and forestall troubles may not destroy civilization, but this failure certainly is destructive of order and socially restrictive. Foreseeing and forestalling require historical judgment and also the understanding and application of ideas. Ideas do have consequences; so does the failure to apply good ideas and judgment in the social order. Knowledge and reason, limited though they may be, are the only defenses of civilization against ignorance and false fear. Together or apart, they give stability and direction to civilization.

In the United States there are at least four major areas in which the application of unsound ideas, or the absence of thoughtful application of principle and of historical judgments, has serious consequences.

The first is the Constitution itself, threatened by an over-eagerness to amend it and interpret it in response to immediate pressures, real or imagined, without regard or attention to the principles and historical experience that underlay the drafting of that document. When the Constitution is amended by a three-fourths approval, that three-fourths places itself in a position of being subsequently held to their position by the one-fourth minority.

The second is the careless disregard for one of the major rights protected by the Constitution, freedom of speech. In particular, we tend to manifest willingness to tolerate and even justify limitations of freedom of speech by a monopoly press which does not understand its function, and to grant to a government agency—the Federal Communications Commission—powers to control culture, including the communication of political information and ideas.

The third concerns another constitutionally guaranteed right, freedom of assembly, which Alexis de Tocqueville said was next in importance in a democratic society to the right of individual liberty. This right is interfered with through the limitation of the right to organize for political purposes. The denial of this right was a principal cause of the American Revolution. The principal instruments through which limitations are imposed are state laws, many of which are unconstitutional, and, since 1974, the Federal Election Campaign Act, executed by the Federal Election Commission, which has been given arbitrary and bureaucratic control over the political processes of the nation.

The fourth is the proliferation of government bureaucracies and the danger that comes of delegating them power. As Frankenstein delegated power to the monster, so do we to impersonal, self-motivated institutions operating on a dynamism of their own. Such bureaucracies differ from one another in their sources of power, modes of operation, and political effects. They range from police and intelligence agencies such the FBI and the CIA, to bureaus and commissions and agencies like the Federal Trade Commission, the Environmental Protection Agency, and the Internal Revenue Service, to the newly established Department of Education.

An ancient Irish law held that society could not take from a person his book, his harp, his sword, or his plow in

settlement of a debt. His book was the repository of knowledge and the sign of his intellectual, moral, and religious
freedom; his harp the instrument of artistic expression; his
sword the sign and agent of his political freedom; and the
plow his means of livelihood, of economic independence.

Why are we threatening to burn our own books, destroy
our harps, break our swords, and let rust the plowshares?

The Constitution

No society can make orderly, consistent progress unless its political policies and programs are reasonably consistent with both philosophical theory and experience.

At the founding of the United States, the three elements, philosophy, policy, and program, were in balance. Thomas Jefferson, John Adams, and their fellow conspirators in the Revolution held a philosophy of government summarized in the Declaration of Independence.

Gilbert Chesterton, in his book *What I Saw in America*, published in 1922, declared, "America is the only nation in the world that is founded on a creed. That creed is set forth with dogmatic and even theological lucidity in the Declaration of Independence; perhaps the only piece of practical politics that is also theoretical politics and also great literature."

The creed, theological and political, to which he referred was expressed in these words of the Declaration: "That all men are created equal; that they are endowed by their Creator with certain unalienable rights; that among these are life, liberty, and the pursuit of happiness. . . ."

These words represent ideas taken seriously by the men who drafted the Declaration. They were not expressed merely as a justification for the Revolution, or as an inspiration, but were intended to persist beyond revolution to become the foundation upon which democratic institutions were built. They were taken seriously because the men who wrote and subscribed to them were in danger of being shot or hanged if the Revolution failed.

There is a growing disposition to accept that the Constitution and the ideas that were built into it have little validity; that they were all right for another time, but need not be respected today.

A typical depreciating statement comes from Stephen Hess of the Brookings Institution, who, in an essay supporting an amendment to the Constitution, justifies it by observing that "the Constitution was written by politicians." Politicians, he then notes, are compromisers and have to settle and satisfy their constituencies.

This is consistent with popular observations of those who would change the Constitution, disregard or circumvent it. The Constitution was, it is true, drafted by a handful of men nearly 200 years ago. They were under political pressure to put forth a document that would receive the support of the number of states necessary for ratification. There were compromises in it, some with principle, as in the recognition of slavery and in the three-fifths compromise by which slaves were counted in the allocation of representation in the Congress. Some were compromises with the realities of power—for example, concessions to the small states as against the large in the allocation of Senate seats.

The men who participated in the drafting of the Constitution acknowledged the reality of compromise and anticipated that not everything they did would stand the test of history.

At the same time, they believed that the principles upon which the new republic was founded were valid and would remain so. They did not look upon what they were undertaking as "the American Experiment," as it is sometimes called, but rather as a test of reason and of historical lessons in a new context.

They did not consider that the intellectual and moral basis for their proposals came from delegates in the convention who were especially gifted or chosen. The principles of government which they introduced at the constitutional convention were as old as political history and philosophy. Thomas Jefferson, George Mason, John Jay, Alexander Hamilton, and others who directly influenced the political thought underpinning the Revolution and the Constitution were not new political thinkers, although most had some new ideas. They were students of politics and of history. They brought with them to the drafting convention the wisdom and the experience of ancient political thinkers as well as those who, by their standards, were due to be considered modern political thinkers.

Plato and Aristotle were at the Convention, as were Montesquieu and *The Spirit of the Laws*, Locke, Hobbes, Adam Smith, and Rousseau.

Plutarch was there as a special resource for both history and political theory, as were the historians Thucydides and Tacitus.

Contemporary, or nearly contemporary, historical sources were used. Jay, for example, in the fifth essay of the *Federalist* papers, quotes from a letter of Queen Anne of England to the Scotch Parliament in which she emphasizes the importance of union between England and Scotland as vital to peace. There are touches of Machiavelli, although he is not identified, and there is the continuing force of biblical thought.

The compelling political force of the Constitution, which has been honored for nearly 200 years, came not from the special gifts of the handful of men who drafted it, or from any special quality of wisdom and integrity existing among the citizens of the thirteen states which ratified and accepted that Constitution, but from its internal strength, based on, and tested in, centuries of thought.

In the 120 years between the adoption of the Constitution (including the ten amendments which comprise the Bill of Rights) and the passage of the Sixteenth Amendment in 1913, the Constitution was amended only five times. Three of those amendments, the Thirteenth, the Fourteenth, and the Fifteenth, were related to the abolition of slavery, the protection of individual rights against state infringement, and the guarantee that the right to vote should not be denied because of race, color, or previous condition of servitude.

Between 1913 and 1971, a period of less than sixty years, the Constitution was amended eleven times. Eleven! Other amendments have been, and are now, under consideration.

The amendments adopted between 1913 and 1971 fall into four categories: first, those that are essentially technical and practical; second, those which, although not absolutely necessary, may be justified on practical grounds as consistent with the principles of the Constitution; third, amendments that do little more than tinker with the Constitution with little justification, either on record or in anticipation of future difficulties; and fourth, those that challenge and change constitutional principles and provisions.

The Sixteenth Amendment, adopted in 1913, was essentially technical and practical. It followed from a Court decision in 1895, in which a divided Supreme Court held that an attempt on the part of Congress in 1894 to tax incomes uniformly throughout the United States was unconstitutional. The Court held that the income tax was a direct tax, which, under the Constitution, had to be apportioned among the states on the basis of population—this despite the fact that in 1881 the Court had unanimously sustained the imposition of a similar tax during the Civil War.

In a series of cases after 1895, the Court, by redefini-

tion of income and other legal devices, began to move
away from the 1895 decision. The Sixteenth Amendment
properly put an end to the uncertainty as to whether the
Court, without a constitutional amendment, would continue
along the lines it was following, gradually rejecting the
1895 decision. The Sixteenth Amendment, it is generally
agreed, conferred no new powers of taxation, but it did
limit the power of Congress to impose taxes free of
court definition. It is likely that if today's income tax had
been anticipated at the time the Constitution was adopted,
a more careful definition of the purpose to which taxes
are put (stated in the Constitution, "to pay the debts
and provide for the common defense and general welfare
of the United States") would have been included.

The Seventeenth Amendment, also adopted in 1913 and
also practical, removed one stage which the Constitution
provided for the selection of senators. The practical justification for the amendment was the evidence of malprac-
tice in the selection of senators by the legislatures. There
were cases of deadlocks in which legislatures left vacancies
unfilled for long periods of time while they waited for new
state elections, or for other developments that might affect
the choice of senators. There was the possibility of corruption: special-interest groups or party factions often
sought to purchase votes or secure political support for
potential senators. There was also popular demand for a
direct vote in the election of senators—a demand justified
in large part because the function of the Senate had greatly
changed in the 125 years since the Constitution was adopted.
Also changed were the responsibilities and the general
political concerns of U.S. senators as distinguished from
state legislators.

When this amendment was under consideration there
was no thought given to changing the existing weighting of

Senate membership in favor of small states. Rather, the amendment formalized recognition of the fact that senators were no longer acting mainly in foreign policy with limited responsibility and in confirming ambassadors, members of the judiciary, and officers of the executive branch. It stated the broader responsibilities for which they are held accountable directly to the electorate.

The Twenty-third Amendment, ratified in 1961, also falls into the category of the technical and practical. It gave to the District of Columbia the right to participate in presidential elections, by assigning to the District a number of presidential electors equal to those to which a state was entitled. The arguments for the amendment were largely those of equity, since the District then had nearly 800,000 people (a number larger than the population of at least eleven states). The amendment did not give the District any of the other attributes of statehood, nor did it change the constitutional powers of Congress to legislate for the District of Columbia.

A grant of representation in Congress (that is, voting rights in both the House of Representatives and the Senate) would have given the District more political power, as would the granting of home rule, not given by statute until 1973.

This was an amendment of minimal consequence, to be faulted on two counts: first, that it did not consider the larger political problems of the District of Columbia, both as to self-government and as to its place in the structure of the federal government; and second, because since it was so minimal in its effect, it encouraged easy tampering with the Constitution, opening the way to superficial amendment, if not disrespect.

In the second category of amendments adopted in this century, those that may not have been absolutely necessary (because of trends in political practice and court decisions) but may be consistent with the spirit and principles of the Constitution are the Nineteenth and the Twenty-sixth.

The Nineteenth Amendment, ratified in 1920, provided that the right to vote shall not be denied or abridged by the United States or by any state on account of sex. This amendment was adopted after sixty years of advocacy (beginning in 1869) by women who had given up on attaining their goal through changing state laws. In fact, there was some agitation for women's suffrage as early as the 1830s, but it was minimal. In 1838, Kentucky authorized and approved the right of women to vote in school elections —an act that was followed by some other states. Then in 1869, Wyoming, as a territory, accorded women suffrage on equal terms with men. When admitted as a state in 1890 it continued the grant. But following that breakthrough there was little progress. By 1914, only ten more states had extended equal voting rights to women.

The constitutional case for the necessity of the Nineteenth Amendment was clearer than that for the current Equal Rights Amendment, since there is some substance to the argument that what is sought by the ERA, in view of recent court decisions, is already largely secured by the Constitution. The counter argument is that whereas this may be true, the process of court actions case by case puts the burden in the wrong place, on those suing for their rights, whereas the adoption of the amendment would place the burden of defense where it should be, and would accelerate the movement toward equal rights for women. In short, the history of the effort to secure the passage of the Nineteenth Amendment argues for the adoption of the Equal Rights Amendment against the gradual process of court cases and modification of federal and state laws.

Of the same order as the Nineteenth Amendment is the Twenty-sixth. Although there was no constitutional bar to extending the vote to persons as young as eighteen, only three states at the time of the adoption of the amendment had done so.

This amendment, adopted in 1971, was a deserving modification. Some critics of it say that the young people have been unappreciative of the new right given to them, and because they have not responded, either in sufficient numbers or in degree of political activism, they have not had any measurable effect on American political life. This may be so, but it does little to prove the case against the amendment, which was, to a large extent, passed to compensate young persons for their abuse during the 1960s, especially during the war in Vietnam.

In any case, persons under twenty-one are voting in fewer numbers than are their elders. This is partly because of the mobility of the young, and partly because of the lack of issues that appeal to them. Had the Twenty-sixth Amendment been passed before the 1968 elections, that political year might have been significantly different from what it was.

The Twenty-fourth Amendment also falls into the practical category. It outlawed the poll tax in federal elections. It is quite likely that the Supreme Court would have held the poll tax unconstitutional in federal elections, as it did in the case of the state poll taxes subsequently, without statute or constitutional amendment.

The argument in support of the amendment was that, since the Congress was not given power under the Constitution to establish or alter qualifications for voting for electors for President and Vice-President, elimination of the poll tax as a requirement for participation in elections was attainable only by constitutional amendment. In any case, the passage of the amendment did no harm to the Constitution.

The third category of amendments includes those that

involved tinkering with the Constitution. The Twentieth, the Twenty-second, and the Twenty-fifth fall into this grouping.

The first of these, the Twentieth Amendment, was proposed by Congress in March 1932. It provided for changing the date for the inauguration of the newly elected President from March to January and eliminated the "lame duck" session of Congress. By January 1933, only ten months after the introduction of the amendment, ratification by the necessary number of states was completed, and on February 6, 1933, the amendment was officially certified as part of the Constitution. Franklin Roosevelt, after his reelection in 1936, was the first United States President to take the oath in January rather than in the March following the national election. While a case might have been made for eliminating the "lame duck" Congress, a better date for the new Congress to begin might have been the end of November of the election year, or as soon after the election as possible. Moreover, there were no instances of obstruction or of serious irresponsibility in the record of "lame duck" Congresses. Nor had "lame duck" Presidents abused the power of the office between the January date prescribed in the amendment and the old March 4 date established by Congress in 1792. There was no serious frustration among newly elected Presidents who were kept out of the office for more than three months after they had been elected. The historical record suggests that the amendment was something of an accident. Possibly Congress, unable or unwilling to do much more about the Depression of 1932, struck upon the idea of a constitutional amendment as a distraction or diversion.

The possibility that if no candidate for President received a majority of the electoral votes, the election, when thrown (or carried) into the House, would be decided by a House of Representatives (chosen in an election preceding the undecided presidential election) deserved some consideration, although, here again, there was nothing on record to indicate that the republic had suffered because of its earlier constitutional provision. This possibility could have been taken care of by a much more limited amendment.

One significant and undesirable consequence of the adoption of the Twentieth Amendment is that newly elected Presidents, instead of having four months during which to prepare to take over the executive branch of the government, are allowed little more than two months. Franklin Roosevelt, before he took over the office, had had approximately 120 days between the election and the beginning of his "first 100 days." Subsequently, newly elected Presidents have had only about 75 days. A four-month delay between election and taking office is not an unreasonable one. Presidents-elect need time to cool off after the campaign. They can use the time to turn aside pressure to make decisions. The longer period would also give more time for the selection of cabinet members and officials of the executive branch.

A second tinkering amendment that has served no real good is the Twenty-second, ratified in 1951. The amendment was initiated by the 80th Congress, one Republican-controlled for the first time since the Hoover administration. The purpose, as stated in the report filed in 1947 in the House of Representatives, was as follows:

"By reason of the lack of a positive expression upon the subject of the tenure of the office of President, and by reason of a well-defined custom which has risen in the past that no President should have more than two terms in that office, much discussion has resulted upon this subject. Hence it is the purpose of this [proposal] to submit this question to the people so they, by and through the recognized processes, may express their views upon this question, and if they shall so elect, they may . . . set at rest this problem."

The explanation is largely nonsense. There had not been much discussion except among those who had opposed Roosevelt's third and fourth terms. And there was no problem to be set at rest. It was adopted as a way of getting even with Franklin Roosevelt after he died. The bearing of the amendment on the presidency is yet to be fully tested. Early evidence is that it should not have been adopted. There have been slight indications that Presidents have begun to think that they have an obligation to serve two terms, if they do not in fact have a right to a second term. *The consequence of this attitude is that a President in office will be most careful to assure his reelection to a second term.* This is a prescription for two irresponsible presidential terms: the first because of the overriding concern of the President to be reelected, and the second because he cannot again be held answerable to the electorate.

The third tinkering amendment of the century was the Twenty-fifth. This one deals with presidential disability and presidential succession. It was ratified in 1967 and was brought on as a consequence of congressional reflections prompted by the medical history of Presidents Kennedy, Eisenhower, and Johnson. The health of Woodrow Wilson and of Franklin Roosevelt was also added to the consideration. Most of the problems, real and supposed, that were the basis for this amendment could have been better handled by statute or left to the wisdom of Congress and cabinet members—and wives or husbands of Presidents.

The first section of the amendment repeats the constitutional provision that, in case of removal of the President from office, or upon his death or resignation, the Vice-President shall become President.

The second section provides that when there is a vacancy in the office of Vice-President, the President shall nominate a Vice-President who shall take his office upon confirmation by a majority vote of both houses of Congress. This procedure could have been handled by statute. Nixon's choice of Gerald Ford to be Vice-President following the resignation of Spiro Agnew, and the approval of President Ford's choice of Nelson Rockefeller to be Vice-President when Ford succeeded to the presidency, indicates that congressional approval is likely to be almost automatic—a response that scarcely warranted a constitutional amendment to define the process of selection.

It is the third section and those following, however, that are most subject to question and objection. The third section provides that the President can transmit to the Congress a written declaration that he is unable to discharge the powers and duties of his office. Following the transmittal of the letter, the powers and duties of the presidency will be discharged by the Vice-President as acting President until the President sends another letter to Congress saying that he is ready to resume the duties of the office to which he was elected.

There are at least three things wrong with this provision. The first is that a President, for political or other reasons, may not want to take such formal action when temporarily disabled. Second, he may not wish to transfer the power to his Vice-President, especially if the Vice-President has been picked as a running mate to balance the ticket. Eisenhower, for example, would certainly have preferred to transfer his powers to someone other than his Vice-President (if reports of their relationship are reasonably accurate). The same, without straining speculation, could be said of the Kennedy-Johnson relationship.

The proposal also lends itself to political exploitation when considered in the light of the two-term limitation on presidential office-holding. A President who is only slightly disabled might disqualify himself several months before the end of his term in order that his Vice-President may take over the office and be able then to present himself as an incumbent, experienced candidate for election to the presidential office. The amendment makes no provision for congressional determination as to whether the President is in fact unable to discharge the powers and duties of his office, or whether he should be allowed to resign for reasons of health solely by his own decision.

The fourth section of the amendment is even more confusing and perhaps dangerous. It prescribes a complicated procedure whereby the Vice-President and a majority of the principal officers of the executive departments—or of a body chosen by the two houses—may transmit to Congress their written declaration that the President is unable to discharge the powers and duties of his office, at which point the Vice-President shall become Acting President.

Thereafter, the President can transmit to the Congress his written declaration that no inability exists and he shall resume the office unless the Vice-President and a majority of the previously described body of officers transmit to Congress within four days a contrary declaration that the President is unable to discharge the powers and duties of the office. Thereupon, Congress shall decide the issue, having assembled within forty-eight hours if not already in session. Within twenty-one days after receipt of the last written declaration, Congress shall act. If by a two-thirds vote of both houses it is determined that the President is unable to discharge the powers and duties of the office, the Vice-President shall continue to carry out the duties. If the vote is less than two-thirds, the President shall resume the powers and duties of his office.

The possibilities for mischief and confusion in this amendment are almost beyond imagination. A President who is fit to exercise the duties of his office could be prey to his Vice-President's claim that he is not fit and so seek to win cabinet support to remove the President from office.

A deposed President could, according to the amendment, ask Congress to reinstate him, thus repeatedly triggering the twenty-one-day rule for congressional action. Whether or not a Vice-President were sincere in believing the President to be disabled, he or she would be subject to suspicion. The presidency could become like the papacy during the Avignon period, or like the crown of England during the War of Roses.

The men who drafted the Constitution assumed that reasonable and responsible men could, within the range of constitutional provisions for impeachment, if necessary, and by statutory accommodation, take care of possible crises such as those imagined as justification for the Twenty-fifth Amendment. Not so the activist constitutional amenders of 1967.

The Eighteenth Amendment, prohibiting the manufacture, sale, or transportation of intoxicating liquors, went into effect in 1920. It was repealed by the Twenty-first Amendment in 1933. The experience of the country with the avoidance of the law, the enfeebled enforcement, and the general disorder should have been anticipated when the amendment was proposed and acted upon. That experience should serve as a lesson against trying to establish morality by constitutional amendment when it is difficult, if not impossible, to do so by law. This amendment was the clearest departure from principle and tradition of constitutional government in America. Whereas the participants in the constitutional convention talked about the desirability (in fact, not the necessity) of a reasonable level of morality in the country and especially in those who held public office, there was no serious attempt to set moral standards in the Constitution.

Currently, the Congress or the state legislatures are considering or being asked to consider four constitutional amendments representative of the four types of amendment that have been acted upon in the past.

One amendment proposes to grant full voting representation in Congress to the District of Columbia. Whereas the states admitted after the Constitution was adopted could be admitted by enabling legislation, the same is not possible for the District, because this is prohibited in the Constitution. The case for giving the District voting representation is a mixed one. The arguments in support of it are the same ones given for the passage of the Twenty-third Amendment, which allowed District citizens to vote in presidential elections, and its adoption will probably be settled on political grounds, as was the controversy over statehood for Alaska and Hawaii.

An amendment in the second category, those not absolutely necessary but justified on practical grounds and also consistent with constitutional principles, is the Equal Rights Amendment. Passage of the amendment would certainly do no violence to the principles of the Constitution, and it would be consistent with actions such as the adoption of the Nineteenth Amendment providing for universal women's suffrage, the Twenty-sixth Amendment extending the vote to persons over eighteen, and the Twenty-fourth Amendment outlawing poll taxes in federal elections.

One amendment not yet acted upon by Congress but nonetheless actively supported is the Human Life (anti-abortion) Amendment. It involves a much more compelling and complex moral issue than did the Eighteenth Amendment. In substance it is of the same order: namely, an amendment that attempts to deal with a controversial and very difficult moral issue.

The general rule that must be applied to governmental intervention in morality is that the object of the action is clearly a threat to social order and stability. If it is not, it remains outside the jurisdiction of the government as far as even statutory regulation might be applied. Certainly a matter of this kind should not be made a constitutional issue. If the object of the action is nominally a threat to society, such as alcohol consumption, an attempt to control its use should be made by statute rather than by constitutional amendment. The social consequences of abortion have not been objectively determined. Arguments for opposing abortion and for advocating both legislative proscription and constitutional bars are based on principle, simply stated as the Right to Life. Abortion is said by some anti-abortionists to be the equivalent of murder. Pro-abortionists deny the charge, obviously, and some of them argue that whereas on a broad scale the advantages, the benefits, or the harm of abortion cannot be demonstrated, it can be demonstrated in particular cases as being good for a family, a mother, or even a community. The arguments range from points of theology to details of physiology, from social good to economic benefits, from high principle to saving taxpayers' money.

The second point to be satisfied before constitutional action is justified is whether it is possible for the government effectively to control a practice as personal and as private as abortion. It is difficult to trust anyone, whether supporter or opponent of abortion, who believes that control could be very effective. Anti-abortionists say that such control would be greatly advanced with the passage of a constitutional amendment banning abortion, and with appropriate statutory punishment to support the amendment.

The third point to be considered is whether, in view of the widespread practice of abortion, a constitutional or statutory ban would make things worse rather than better, with abortion operations taken out of hospitals and performed by illegal or unqualified practitioners or by women themselves.

The one sure conclusion is this: a matter of this kind

should not be made the substance of a *constitutional* amendment.

The fourth kind of constitutional amendment, that involving tinkering with the Constitution and its principles and procedures without good reason, is the amendment proposed to change the method of electing the President of the United States.

Concern over the process of electing the President and over the operation of the electoral college is not new. Nearly every Congress since the beginning of the nineteenth century has considered some proposal to revise the method by which the President and the Vice-President are chosen. The reforms generally propose one or more basic plans for change. The "district plan" would have electors chosen not on a statewide winner-take-all basis, but by districts, congressional or other. Such a plan was passed by the Senate in 1813 but was not acted on by the House of Representatives. The "proportional plan," first introduced in 1848, would allocate electoral votes according to the popular votes cast within the state. Thus Republicans, Democrats, Independents, and others might share the electoral votes from a particular state.

Another plan was the "direct election" of the President by popular vote, first proposed in 1816. This latter method of electing the President was the subject of prolonged consideration at the constitutional convention—a consideration marked by clear disagreement among the delegates. In the course of that consideration, various procedures were proposed; some were adopted, then rejected. In the first series of votes on the issue, according to Roger MacBride's book *The American Electoral College* (based largely on Madison's journal of the 1787 convention), the question of direct election by the people was defeated by a vote of nine states to one. Then the question of electors chosen by the state legislatures was moved and was beaten down by a vote they were committed, with one or two irrelevant exceptions.

Advocates of a constitutional amendment base their case principally on two arguments. One is the case of the "faithless elector" who might vote for someone other than the candidate to whom he is pledged. This has happened only a few times in history—usually involving a protest by one elector. The prevailing custom, sustained in a number of states by a pledge or oath and in other states by law, requiring the elector to vote for the candidate of the party the elector represents is well established. It is quite likely that if the outcome of a presidential election depended on holding an elector faithful, the courts would require faithfulness.

What seems to have agitated the reformers most is the possibility that, under the present system, a presidential candidate who comes in second in the popular vote can win the presidency. This is not surprising; nor should it be shocking. The weighting of the allocation of electors, by giving every state, large and small, two electors more than the number of members the state had in the House of Representatives, was an implicit recognition of this possibility. In fact, if the weighting were not to have any influence, that is, not to have the potential to elect a candidate who receives the smaller popular vote, there would have been no point in the weighting itself. It borders on the ridiculous to announce in a kind of panic, nearly 200 years after the Constitution was adopted, that something that was contemplated could take place, and has in fact taken place.

It is suggested by alarmists that an election in which the winner received fewer votes than the loser would bring on a constitutional crisis; a President might be elected by electors from states whose total voting population was less than that of states voting for the winner. Such an election might bring on a crisis, although there is nothing on the record to suggest that it would. In any event, it would not be a constitutional crisis.

Candidates finishing second have twice been elected to the presidency: Rutherford B. Hayes in 1876 and Benjamin Harrison in 1888. There was no crisis in either year. In the case of Hayes, the issues that might have created a crisis were the difference of one electoral vote as well as disputed elections. The issue was *not* that the accepted count gave the majority of votes to Samuel J. Tilden. The election was settled by a commission set up to study it by a straight party vote, and then was upheld in the Senate again by a straight party vote. As a result Hayes was declared the winner, with a count of 185 electoral votes to 184.

Advocates of direct popular election cite the close calls in recent years. They note that there is grave doubt as to whether John Kennedy or Richard Nixon received the larger popular vote in 1960. That is true, and there are doubts as to whether the results might have been different in the electoral college if vote counts had been more accurate. Yet there was no national crisis.

Again, in the more recent election of 1976, the alarmists observe that a shift of roughly 9,000 votes in Ohio and Hawaii, rather disparate areas of the United States, would have given an electoral victory to Gerald Ford, even though he would have trailed Carter by nearly 2 million popular votes. It is not likely that there would have been a national crisis if this had taken place.

Out of all this has come a constitutional amendment that proposes direct election of the President by popular vote, which method, it is argued, would eliminate all uncertainty as to legitimacy and would preclude constitutional or political crises that could arise under existing procedures. An additional argument is that the direct elections could sustain and strengthen the two-party system. The

League of Women Voters evidently assumes that this is good in itself, for as a League witness said in hearings before the Senate Subcommittee on the Constitution, some people "argue that direct election, in fact, can be the glue that would hold the major political parties together."

Similarly, another witness argued that "a peripheral advantage to the direct-election plan would be an invigoration of the floundering two-party system in the United States." Why the Constitution should be amended to invigorate a "floundering two-party system" is not made clear, especially in view of the fact that the Constitution was conceived as a document that would compensate for party excesses, if it could not altogether eliminate them. John Adams observed some 200 years ago, in anticipation of the adoption of a Constitution similar to that which was adopted for the United States, that the development of a political system dominated by two strong parties or factions would be the worst of all possibilities. Now, what he foresaw as the *worst* development is to be fostered by constitutional amendment, with the argument that the direct-election method would relieve the major parties of having to make concessions to a third party to gain sufficient electoral votes to reach a majority. Evidently, all compromises are to be made between two major parties, and other political influence is to be nullified by legal, even constitutional, exclusion.

Advocates of the direct-election amendment also argue that direct election would honor the principle of "one person, one vote." It would, but only if one accepts and advocates a wider application of that principle than the Supreme Court intended. The Court has not held, for example, that the manner in which United States senators are elected is invalid because senators from small states represent fewer persons than do those from larger states. The one-person-one-vote principle was applied by the Court only within jurisdictions in which every citizen and every vote were held to be legally equal. If the advocates of this position, principally the League of Women Voters, wish to make this argument, they should be consistent and oppose the constitutional provisions that weight the voting strength of small states, not only in the electoral college but also in the election of the Senate.

Of all the proposals for changing the method of electing the President, the direct-election proposal is probably the worst in its possible effects on politics, on representative government, on better selection of Presidents, and in its disregard, if not rejection, of the wisdom of the men who drafted the Constitution.

A compromise proposition, which respects the traditional constitutional provisions for the use of electors but seeks to eliminate the possibility that a presidential candidate who receives a smaller popular vote than his opponent might be elected, was developed in 1978 by a task force of the Twentieth Century Fund. The heart of the task force proposal was the recommendation of a national pool of electoral votes that would be added to the pool of electoral votes in the existing procedure for choosing electors. The national pool would be made up of two electoral votes for each state (plus the District of Columbia) and would be awarded on a winner-take-all basis to the candidate with the most popular votes in the national election. These bonus electoral votes would be added to the state pools, and the candidate with the majority of electoral votes would be elected President. Using the national bonus would virtually eliminate the possibility of defeat for the winner of the popular vote.

But in the task force proposal, as was the case among witnesses supporting the Direct Election Amendment, strengthening the two-party system is introduced as a sustaining reason for the provisions of the amendment. The argument is that with the 102 bonus votes going to the candidate receiving the largest popular vote, the possibility of a third party's influencing the outcome of a presidential election would be all but eliminated. This is an obvious repudiation of an earlier statement by the task force that the amendment would encourage healthy competition through a strong two-party system without unduly restricting the development of third parties. How it would stimulate two-party competition is not as clear as is the way in which it would all but eliminate the influence of third parties and hence discourage, if not directly restrict, their development. Hopelessness and frustration are discouraging even if not entirely restrictive.

Neither the direct-election proposal nor the hybrid proposed by the Twentieth Century Fund task force meets the real need. Both are defective in that they are not based on the right or original conception of how Presidents should be chosen. The trouble with the electoral college is not the conception of it, but that it has not been used as it was intended.

The original conception was that electors would be chosen for one task only, a very important one in the new republic: the selection of a President of the United States. As electors they were to be agents of the people of their states. It was anticipated that the electors would be wise and responsible, that they would be more free of involvement with politics and legislative matters because they were not members of Congress or of state legislatures. The electoral college, as it was called, was designed to deny both Congress and the voters total and direct power over the election. Whereas the Founding Fathers knew what political factions were—division being the mark of every political society—they hoped and believed that these divisive and power-seeking organizations would have a limited influence in the choice of members of Congress and especially of the President.

In assessing the relative merits of proposed constitutional amendments concerning the electoral college, the only worthwhile consideration is whether the amendments will make for fuller participation by the people in the choice of the President. Will voters participate more fully, not just in absolute numbers and in percentages, but also, following the election, will they accept a choice that has been made which represents, directly or indirectly, the majority judgment of the people? This is the important question.

The present procedures give no such assurance, nor would the proposal for the direct election of the President currently given most support by the Senate Judiciary Committee. The Maine system, by which one electoral vote goes to the winner of the popular vote in each congressional district and two electoral votes go to the winner of the state-wide popular vote, is clearly better than the winner-take-all rule applied in the other forty-nine states. Better than the Maine district system would be one dividing the states into presidential electoral districts, each smaller than a congressional district, which now includes about 450,000 persons.

If each presidential elector represented, say, a district of 100,000 persons, a candidate for the electoral college could campaign effectively without spending great sums of money for campaign activities. One person with a few volunteers could, in the course of a presidential campaign, reach all voters in his 100,000-person constituency. If the country were divided into some 2,000 such districts, 2,000 presidential electors would be chosen. Obviously, if a majority of those chosen were Democrats, a Democratic President would be chosen; if a majority were Republicans, a Republican would be President. If neither party had a majority, the third- or fourth-party electors would hold the balance of power and their votes would have to be solicited by other parties.

This procedure is no different from the one followed within U.S. political parties at their conventions (or on the way to conventions). In Great Britain in the choice of Prime Minister, under the parliamentary system, it is used.

A President chosen through this process would clearly be a constitutional President, and he would be chosen by electors who represented a majority, if not of the voters, almost certainly of the citizens.

This system would make unnecessary the contrived party quota system being tested within the Democratic party, since no measure of gerrymandering could effectively exclude minorities from fair representation. In fact, if one assumes that electoral districts of approximately 100,000 persons are established, electors chosen would be roughly proportionate in numbers to the minority groups existing in the national population. This would be more effective and fairer representation than that achieved by minorities under existing practice which limits their political influence to participation in conventions and in the general elections. Under this procedure, the impact of minorities would be felt at the most critical and important point of decision: the selection of a President.

Better than the present practice, and also better than the direct-election proposal of the Senate Judiciary Committee, would be the adoption of a system similar to that proposed in the Lodge-Gossett Amendment of the 1950s: the apportionment of electoral votes within each state on the basis of the number of votes gained by the electors, or the candidate whom they supported. This procedure would emphasize state differences and would permit and encourage local political efforts over nationwide campaigns.

Curiously, politicians, political commentators, and political scientists approve in the proceedings of political parties the very things which they see as most dangerous, undemocratic, and unrepresentative in the electoral college. Democrats who now advocate the winner-take-all direct national election since 1968 have favored proportionate representation at the Democratic National Convention. They outlawed the unit rule in state delegations. Before the convention of 1976, they outlawed the winner-take-all state primary as a way of choosing delegates to the national convention. The Republicans seem to be moving in the same direction. The quota system reflects a concern not to eliminate persons (or points of view) early in the pre-convention process, but rather to keep them active (or demonstrable) up to a point of final party choice. Yet the Democrats now hold this same principle to be dangerous if applied in the selection of the President.

Reconciliation of differences, even compromises, is acceptable in conventions run by political parties, but compromise and reconciliation by a national assembly—the electoral college—are supposed to be dangerous.

Delegates sent to party conventions, even when chosen in party primaries, are usually held to the commitment established by the primary only up to a point, after which they are free to support candidates other than the one they were associated with in the primary election. At conventions, delegations or delegates often finally support candidates other than those whom they were chosen to support.

In many parliamentary governments, the choice of Prime Minister involves compromise, negotiations, and concessions—not at conventions but at the point of final choice.

The choice is this: if we assume that the electoral process and the electoral college are not working well, we should *one*, change the process substantially, as the Senate Judiciary Amendment proposes (recommending direct election of the President), or *two*, make the electoral college work better. As J. H. Dougherty said as long ago as 1906, "To try to restore the electoral scheme of the fathers would be a chimerical undertaking. To attempt the creation of any plan in conflict with the plain trend of institutional development would be equally unwise." Or we should follow the advice of another student of American politics of about the same period, John Holcombe, who argued that "in no reactionary spirit, therefore, but with views thoroughly progressive," we should "return for relief to the wisdom of the fathers by making effective their admirable device—the electoral college."

In so speaking, he sustained the judgment of Madison, not only as expressed in the Constitution, but as late as 1823, when he wrote, "One advantage of electors is, that although generally the mere mouths of their constituents, they may be intentionally left sometimes, to their own judgment, guided by further information that may be acquired of them; and finally, what is of material importance, they will be able, when ascertaining which may not be till a late hour, that the first choice of their constituents is utterly hopeless, to substitute in the electoral college the name known to be their second choice."

Consistent with Madison's view, one slate of North Carolina electors in 1824 was pledged to both Andrew Jackson and John Quincy Adams, with the understanding that they would vote for the one who had the best chance of winning—an understanding that is often carried to conventions by delegates. In 1912 the Teddy Roosevelt ticket of electors generally declared that if Roosevelt could not be elected and if the contest became one of Taft versus Wilson, they would vote for Taft.

The need for purifying and perfecting the process of the selection of the President is most important at this time, because of the complexity and weight of the demands of

the presidential office, and because voter knowledge of the
qualifications of the presidential candidates is obscured or
distorted with the intrusion of media hype. Yet it is better to
improve the representative process, as conceived by Madison, than to propose that it should be done away with
because the representative process has not worked in an
electoral college. The problem is not the defects in the
conception of that constitutional institution but, rather, it
is the intrusion of partisanship and the intervention of
political parties and conventions between the people and
the electoral college.

Over the last few years, a much-publicized drive for
another constitutional amendment has arisen, causing concern among traditional defenders of constitutional purity
and even some concern among the more ready amenders of
the Constitution, both in and outside Congress. To be
formulated at a new constitutional convention, the proposed amendment would require that, under conditions not
yet clearly specified, the budget of the federal government
must be balanced each year. The necessary preliminary
action for calling such a convention is under way in the
state legislatures. The motivations of the state legislatures
are mixed. Some, one can believe, do want the federal
government's budget balanced. In other cases, support for
the convention and for the amendment is an obvious response to political pressures by men who should stand
against it. Still other legislatures, including those that have
been unable to balance their own state budgets, back the
amendment in a demonstration of the "Never on Sunday"
principle. They hope voters will excuse state imbalances or
at least be distracted from home realities.

The "Balance the Budget" amendment is, of course, ridiculous and dangerous and should not be adopted. But
the fact that it has moved so far along the way to con-

sideration should not be blamed solely on the state legislators and public sponsors. The Congress and the executive
branch have encouraged the budget-balancing efforts by
being irresponsible in federal fiscal affairs. This alone is not
a force strong enough to move state legislators and citizens
to act as they have. Along the way, the Congress, with
presidential support, has done things suggesting that federal finances cannot be controlled in a rational and orderly
way. For over thirty years, Congress has followed a policy
of passing resolutions setting ceilings on the national debt.
Currently the resolutions set two debt ceilings, one dis-
couragingly labeled the "permanent debt ceiling" and the
other more optimistically called the "temporary debt ceiling."

In 1947 the permanent ceiling was set at $275 billion. In
1955 the permanent ceiling held at the $275 billion mark,
but the temporary ceiling was set at $281 billion. Dur-
ing most of the Kennedy-Johnson years the permanent
ceiling was set at $285 billion, while the temporary ceiling
ranged from $8 to $51 billion above that base. In the
Nixon-Ford years, the permanent limitation on the debt
was set at $400 billion, a good round number, but the
temporary ceiling ranged $50 to $282 billion above the
permanent ceiling. The combined permanent and temporary borrowing authority is now in the area of $880 billion.

The only clear result of imposing ceilings is that federal
borrowing has been made increasingly complicated and
sometimes more expensive. To supplement the ineffective
debt-ceiling resolutions, Congress recently approved a
program by which two congressional budget committees
are set up, one for the Senate and one for the House of
Representatives. The reason given for the additional staff
and effort was that if each congressional body had its own
budget, the overall view of the national budget would be

clearer and therefore it would be possible to bring governmental expenditures under better control—perhaps even balance the budget.

More recently, Congress has issued a directive to the President that he must submit for the executive branch of the government two budgets—one balanced and the other unbalanced—unless, possibly, he wanted to submit one balanced budget.

State legislators and others have been encouraged to go the constitutional amendment route, not only because Congress and Presidents have shown that they cannot control the budget, but also because of the readiness of Congress and Presidents to propose different constitutional amendments, some of little merit, others ill-conceived and even dangerous.

What is needed to protect the Constitution is someone like Joe Rollette, who was a member of the territorial legislature of Minnesota in 1857.

In that year, the year before Minnesota won statehood, the territorial legislature passed a bill that would have moved the capital (once statehood was granted) from Saint Paul, the site of the territorial government, to the city of Saint Peter. It was known that the so-called Removal Bill would be signed by the territorial governor, who was sympathetic to the Saint Peter site. Enter Joe Rollette, chairman of the Committee on Enrolled Bills of the territorial legislature. With the Removal Bill in his possession, Joe went into hiding for a week. Some historians say that he hid out in the swamp near Saint Paul now known as Pig's Eye Lake. Others say that he spent the week in more comfortable surroundings, playing poker with cronies. In either case, Joe did not turn up with the bill until the end of the legislative term, when it was too late for the governor to sign it.

Rollette's portrait is prominently displayed on a wall of

the Minnesota Club in Saint Paul. Saint Peter, as a consolation for having lost the capital designation and the state government, was given the state's first mental institution.

If Joe were about Washington today, he might be encouraged, each time the amenders approached the Constitution, to snatch the document and keep it in hiding until it was safe to bring it out again.

Federal Election Control, Phase One

The most serious obstacle to the exercise of the political right of freedom of assembly which is basic to American democracy is intervention by the Federal Election Campaign Act Amendments enacted in 1974 and largely approved by the Supreme Court in 1976.

Although, over the years, proposals have been made for federal intervention in political processes, most such proposals were wisely rejected. Article I, Section 4, of the Constitution provides: "The times, places and manner of holding elections for Senators and Representatives, shall be prescribed in each State by the Legislature thereof; but the Congress may at any time by law make or alter such regulations, except as to the places of choosing Senators." This provision has been honored.

The Constitution makes slight reference to the process by which Presidents are to be elected. It gives Congress no control over such elections, except for allowing Congress to determine the time of choosing electors and the time for electors to cast their ballots.

In the early history of the country the states followed a variety of presidential electoral procedures. Not until the twentieth century was there any significant or effective move to involve the federal government in presidential politics. The first attempt at campaign regulation and control by the federal government was made in the early 1900s, when President Theodore Roosevelt proposed a system of public funding of federal elections and a prohibition of corporate campaign contributions. His public funding proposal was not adopted, but in 1907 Congress did adopt the Tillman Act, which prohibited national banks and corporations chartered by Congress from making campaign contributions. A Court case in 1957 explained the purpose of the 1907 act, saying that it was "not merely to prevent the subversion of the integrity of the electoral process," but "to sustain the active, alert responsibility of the individual citizen in a democracy for the wise conduct of government." Evidently, the Court believed that if corporations were permitted to contribute, individuals would be discouraged from doing so.

In 1909, an attempt was made to broaden the 1907 act to include contributions of all items of value, and to cover state legislative races as well. That effort failed, but in 1910 Congress passed the first disclosure law. All contributions in excess of $100 to and by political committees had to be disclosed, and expenditures in excess of $50 made outside political committees had to be reported.

In 1911 ceilings of $5,000 and $10,000 respectively were placed on House and Senate campaign expenditures. In 1918 Congress set criminal penalties for offering money to influence voting. There is only one case of prosecution on record under these laws. In 1921 Truman Newberry was convicted of exceeding the expenditure ceiling in his 1918 Michigan senate primary race. His conviction was reversed and the major provisions of the law were judged to be unconstitutional by the Supreme Court, on the grounds that primaries were intra-party affairs, and that Congress could not limit expenses under such conditions.

Reform lapsed until 1925, when Congress passed the Federal Corrupt Practices Act. In a case in 1934 the Supreme Court upheld that act, justifying the law in these

Machiavellian words: "If it can be seen that the means adopted are really calculated to attain the end, the degree of their necessity, the extent to which they conduce to the end, the closeness of the relationship between the means adopted and the end to be attained, are matters for congressional determination alone."

With a dexterity of language that antedates Marshall McLuhan, who coined the expression "the medium is the message," the Court pointed out that methods, if close to the ends, become in fact indistinguishable from them. It continued, "Congress reached the conclusion that public disclosure of political contributions, together with the names of contributors and other details, would tend to prevent corrupt use of money to affect elections. The verity of this conclusion reasonably cannot be denied." Neither could it be proved.

The Court added that "it seems plain that the statute as a whole is calculated to discourage the making and use of contributions for purposes of corruption." The Court asserted that Congress undoubtedly possesses power under the Constitution to "preserve the departments and institutions of the general government from impairment or destruction, whether threatened by force or by corruption." This is a broad grant of power, for deciding what constitutes corruption and who is corrupt requires a highly subjective judgment, as does the decision about what constitutes impairment of the government and of its departments.

The late thirties and the early forties saw a new surge of legislative efforts to control elections. In 1939 Congress passed the Hatch Act, which banned overt political activities in federal elections by all federal employees except presidential appointees. In 1940 Congress limited spending by political committees to $3 million and limited gifts to candidates or political committees to $5,000 in any one calendar year.

In 1941 the Supreme Court held that the regulatory powers of Congress extended to primary elections. This case overruled the old *Newberry* ruling, which had eliminated primaries from regulation. Labor union political activities were brought under federal regulation in 1943 and were kept there under provisions of the Taft-Hartley Act of 1947.

These laws did not work very well because there were so many ways of avoiding them, in expenditures and contributions, and they were largely ignored in practice.

In 1962 President Kennedy's Presidential Commission on Campaign Costs proposed tax incentives and tax credits for small political contributions, more realistic ceilings on campaign expenditures, and the suspension of the equal-time provisions of the Federal Communications Act for media debates. It is not unusual for Presidents to recommend campaign reform *after* they are elected.

In 1966 Congress provided for a one-dollar checkoff on income-tax returns to provide money for public financing in presidential elections, but that law was suspended before the 1968 elections. Although it was revived by Congress in 1971, implementation of the checkoff plan was again delayed. Also in 1971, three years after the election of Richard Nixon, Congress passed another law, the Federal Election Campaign Act of 1971, requiring the disclosure of all contributions in excess of $100, of spending by all candidates, and of spending by committees that spent more than $1,000 per year. The act put expenditure ceilings only on media advertising. This provision incorporated into law the dubious principle that the use of the most effective means of communication should be limited.

Thus, through the maze of contradictions, of confusing Court decisions, of congressional twistings and turnings, and of reversals, the country was brought to the year 1974—the year of reform. This was a year in which Congress attempted, through amalgamation, to accomplish all that it had been unable to do through separate, more restrained, and better-defined efforts over a period of nearly seventy years. Thus, it honored a legislative principle which holds that what cannot be done in an orderly way may be accomplished through totality, by consolidated and comprehensive laws.

In 1974 the times were right for the reformers. Watergate was part of history, and whereas the country was not as shocked by it as the press reported, or as politicians (especially liberal Republicans and Democrats) said, the experience was disturbing enough to cause near-panic in the Congress and to set up what Senator Eugene Millikin of Colorado used to call an "antelope situation." When pressed for an explanation, the senator explained that it was a situation in which there was nothing to do, except "to paint a white stripe down the seat of one's pants and to go over the hill running with the antelope."

Under these conditions, and urged on by such purifiers as Common Cause and the League of Women Voters, Congress passed the Federal Election Campaign Act Amendments of 1974. Then, when the reformers were ready to attack anyone who opposed the legislation as a defender of Richard Nixon and of the whole Watergate experience, opposition required the kind of heroic virtue that theologians say should not be asked of anyone but a saint.

The Federal Election Campaign Act Amendments of 1974, as reported to the Senate, limited to $3,000 the amount that any individual could contribute to any candidate's campaign in any federal election. They also provided that the public would help finance all elections, including the House and Senate races, out of the U.S. Treasury. They also limited the amount the candidate could spend from all sources in each election.

In primaries, a candidate for President was limited to

spending ten cents for each person of voting age, or approximately $14 million. Apparently what the country needed was a good ten-cent voter. In general elections, voters were either worth more or could cost more, for the proposal allowed a candidate to spend fifteen cents times the Voting Age Population (VAP), which came to $21 million, for a national campaign.

Senators were allowed to spend ten cents times the VAP in primaries in their states, and fifteen cents times the VAP in general elections, or $175,000, whichever was higher. House members were limited to ten cents times the VAP or $90,000 in primaries and to $90,000 in general elections. The bill also proposed limits on the amount of personal funds that candidates could spend on their own behalf. For presidential candidates, $50,000; for Senate candidates, $35,000; for House candidates, $25,000.

For violations of the expenditure limits, the fines varied from $1,000 to $25,000, and the term of imprisonment from one to five years. The bill outlawed cash contributions in excess of $100, and cash expenditures in excess of that amount. Also, it strengthened all reporting requirements. Under the bill, every elected federal official had to disclose his or her personal and family financial interests.

Senate debates on election reform began not in the shadow but in the glow of Watergate. In February 1974, the Democratic majority leader, Senator Mike Mansfield, issued the opening battle cry. "We shall not finally come to grips with the problems," he said, "except as we are prepared to pay for the public business of elections with public funds." On April 11 the Senate passed the bill by a 53 to 32 vote, over the opposition of Senator James Buckley and other conservatives.

House debate on the Campaign Reform Bill began on August 7, 1974. By the time that debate began, the House Judiciary Committee had voted articles of impeachment on the President, and the Supreme Court had ruled unanimously that the President had to surrender his tapes to Special Prosecutor Leon Jaworski. The House of Representatives prepared to consider campaign reform legislation under a special rule of debate which provided in effect that important amendments could be offered only by the Committee on House Administration, a committee controlled by Congressman Wayne Hays of Ohio.

In commenting on this rule, one Republican congressman, a member of the House Administration Committee, said, "I thought it was a joke."

Congressman Bill Archer of Texas, another Republican, observed, "Unfortunately, we will not be allowed to offer . . . amendments on the House floor. . . . In my opinion," he continued, "this is an irresponsible answer to the nation's plea for open election processes. The bill that should accomplish that goal has become itself a closed partisan issue. As it now stands, there can be no amendment to restrict the 'in-kind' contributions Democrats enjoy from big labor. Instead, the limitation has actually been increased from $100 provided in present law to $500 per individual. Nor can any amendment even be considered to restrict contributions by organized groups, whether they be big labor or big business, which deny the individual's right to decide which candidate receives his contribution."

On a vote to take up the rule for a vote, the House divided on party lines, with 218 Democrats and 1 Republican voting to take up the rule, and 181 Republicans and 9 Democrats voting against the motion.

One of the first controversies in the House of Representatives was over ceilings on expenditures in elections to the House of Representatives. The committee bill proposed a ceiling of $75,000 in the general election, with an additional 25 percent, or $18,750, allowed for fund-raising expenditures. Eventually the House settled for a $60,000 ceiling for each election. The House also adopted an amendment eliminating provisions for the public financing of national party nominating conventions, but this provision was later restored.

Congressman Bill Frenzel moved to eliminate the provisions of the law for the partial financing of presidential primaries by the government, arguing that public funding would only encourage more and more senators to neglect their duties to run for the presidency every four years.

Representative John Brademas, a Democrat and author of the disputed primary-financing provision, responded to Frenzel by referring to President Nixon, who was expected to announce his resignation later that day—a resignation that had no relationship to public funding of presidential elections. Brademas said that if the Republicans voted against public funding, "the American people will reject them at the polls in November, even as the American people are rejecting the present President of the United States." It mattered not that Nixon had won two years earlier or that, at the time of the Brademas statement, he was being rejected not "at the polls," but "in the polls."

Representative Frenzel's amendment was defeated by a vote of 253 to 163. A motion by Congressman Morris Udall to provide federal financing of congressional elections was defeated 228 to 187. The House then went on to provide that the election law would be enforced by a Board of Supervisory Officers, to be appointed without presidential participation under rules subject to veto by either the House of Representatives or the Senate, again without presidential participation. This proposal setting up new unconstitutional election procedures was adopted by a vote of 391 to 25. The final vote on the bill, on August 8, was 355 to 48. Nixon announced his resignation that evening.

By the time the Senate and the House conferees were appointed and met to work out a compromise bill, Gerald

Ford was President of the United States. With Nixon gone, the conferees agreed to let the President of the United States appoint two of the six members of the proposed Federal Election Commission, thus making the proposal one-third constitutional.

The conferees also eliminated public financing of congressional elections from the bill and limited individual contributions to candidates running for federal office to $1,000 per election in any primary, runoff, or general election. No individual could contribute more than $25,000 per year to all candidates for federal office, but there was no separate limit on the amount an individual could contribute to a political party, as long as it was not earmarked for any named candidate. (In 1976 Congress set a limit of $20,000 per year on the amount an individual could contribute to a political party.)

Political parties, party committees (never well defined), and other political organizations were allowed to contribute not more than $5,000 to each candidate for federal office, or for each primary, runoff, or general election. There were no annual limitations on total donations by political party committees or organizations.

Candidates seeking nomination for the presidency could spend no more than $12 million and were eligible for public funds on a matching one-for-one basis, if they could raise $100,000 in contributions of not more than $250 each, with a minimum of $5,000 from each of twenty states. In the general election, major presidential candidates were limited to expenditures of $20 million, all of which was to be provided from public funds designated through the income-tax checkoff system.

Senate candidates were limited to spending eight cents per voter or $100,000, whichever was greater, in primary elections. Evidently Congress thought that the voters in Senate general elections were worth more, for it allowed a spending limit of twelve cents per voter or $150,000, whichever was higher.

House candidates were limited to $70,000 in primaries and the same amount in general elections. Both House and Senate candidates were allowed to spend an additional 20 percent above the basic limit in raising campaign funds.

Third parties and independent candidates were all but ignored by the law. The major concession was that any third-party candidate (it is still unclear whether this applies to independent candidates) who got over 5 percent of the vote in the general election would be eligible for a pro-rata granting of funds after the election to meet certain undefined debts.

All candidates were subjected to stringent disclosure requirements.

On October 15, Gerald Ford signed the campaign act into law. Although he raised the question of its constitutionality, he felt the courts should decide. The effective date for the Federal Election Campaign Act was January 1, 1975.

On January 2, 1975, a group made up of Senator James Buckley of New York, Stewart Rawlings Mott, the New York Civil Liberties Union, myself, and others joined in filing a suit in the United States District Court of the District of Columbia, asking that the entire act be declared unconstitutional. The suit was called *Buckley* v. *Valeo.*

More specifically, we asked for declaratory and injunctive relief against the provisions of the Federal Election Campaign Act of 1971 and the Federal Election Campaign Amendments of 1974, and Subtitle H of the Internal Revenue Code. The complaint listed thirty-three separate causes of action and attacked virtually every section of the campaign act as violating the Constitution of the United States in one or more respects.

The general grounds for our complaint were that the

statutes denied to some citizens freedom of speech and of association, the right to privacy, and due process and were in violation of the First, Fourth, Fifth, Sixth, and Ninth Amendments to the Constitution.

We argued that the First Amendment rights to freedom of speech were violated by the limitation on contributions and on expenditures, and that the statutes discriminated against challengers and in favor of incumbents in expenditure limits and more generally in the official financing of the two major parties to the practical elimination of all other parties and independent candidates, and thus that they violated fundamental rights of assembly. We argued that the record-keeping and disclosure provisions violated the right of privacy and would, or could, lead to harassment. We also argued that the mode of appointment and confirmation of members of the Federal Election Commission and the power given to it to administer, interpret, and enforce the statutes were in violation of the constitutional provisions for the separation of powers.

Federal Election Control, Phase Two: The Appeals Court

The case—*Buckley* v. *Valeo*—was first brought in the District Court of the District of Columbia on January 2, 1975, and assigned to Judge Howard Corcoran, who, acting under a special judicial review provision in the Federal Election Campaign Act, transmitted the entire case to the U.S. Court of Appeals for the District of Columbia Circuit, sometimes referred to as the court to appeal from. Then, in order to make it possible to appeal to the Supreme Court within a reasonable time, the participants agreed to argue the case relative to twenty-eight constitutional questions or subquestions.

The case was heard by the full appeals court: chief Judge David L. Bazelon, and Judges Skelly Wright, Carl McGowan, Edward A. Tamm, Harold Leventhal, Spottswood W. Robinson III, George E. MacKinnon, and Malcolm R. Wilkey. Our position, in opposing the law, was represented before the court by Brice M. Clagett of Washington, D.C., and Ralph Winter, Jr., of New Haven, Connecticut, with John R. Bolton and Arthur F. Fergenson on the briefs. Joel M. Gora of New York City represented the New York Civil Liberties Union.

The law was defended before the appeals court by Ralph S. Spritzer, special counsel to the Federal Election Commission, with John G. Murphy general counsel, and Paul Bender special counsel to the Federal Election Commission on the brief. Kenneth J. Guido, Jr., supported by Fred Wertheimer, represented John Gardner's Common Cause. Lloyd N. Cutler and others represented the Center for Public Financing of Elections and the League of Women Voters. The attorney general was represented by Dennis G. Linder, a Department of Justice attorney, with support of other attorneys from the Justice Department. These were the principal lawyers involved in the case.

During the proceedings it became clear that the acoustics in the courtroom were bad, or else some judges were hard of hearing. The court first admitted that discourse could not be heard and later requested lawyers to keep their voices up. Since the microphone could not be raised to suit Brice Clagett, who is about six-feet-four, he had to speak from a crouch, which is not the best position from which to address a court. If acoustical arrangements are not changed in the courtroom, it might be advisable for anyone taking a case before the court to be represented only by a short lawyer.

Clagett argued principally that the Federal Election Campaign Act violated the constitutionally guaranteed right of freedom of speech. Political campaigns are, he pointed out, "dependent on . . . contributions, and the expenditure of money. To limit contributions and expenditures is to limit, in every meaningful sense, the speech which they make possible."

He then explained to the court that in the campaign law under review, a candidate who had reached the expenditure limit was prohibited from spending another penny to make his political views known. He could not issue a press release, mail a letter, or hire a secretary to type one. He could not hire a hall to make a speech or make a long-distance telephone call.

It seemed clear to us that unless political campaigning was to be limited to a candidate's talking directly to individual voters, spending money to communicate ideas and positions was integral to the exercise of freedom of speech. Clagett suggested to the court that it consider whether a law limiting the expenditures of a newspaper to x number of dollars per year in order to bring it into line with its competitors, thus restricting it to a smaller number of editions or to fewer inches of print, would not be an infringement on freedom of the press and of speech.

The commitment of this country to freedom of speech and of the press is so strong and so well sustained by court decisions, Clagett said, that the statute that we were challenging should "enjoy no presumption of constitutionality. To the contrary, any law directly inhibiting freedom of expression in the basic crucial area of public debate on public questions, let alone in the area of elections, must come before the courts under a heavy disability." "Seldom, if ever," he added, "has the law ever come before the courts of this country with the reasons for any presumption of constitutionality so wholly absent."

So strong is the constitutional base for freedom of expression that the courts have recognized only in most unusual cases (usually those involving pornography) any compelling need to qualify freedom of communication.

The compelling need for the limitation on contributions and on expenditure, argued the supporters of the legislation, arose from three conditions.

First was the rising cost of campaigns. The law's answer was to limit expenditure without regard for the fact that in consequence of the limitation, communications would also be limited. By extension, one might have argued that even though costs were not high, politicians were communicating too much, taking space in the press and time on radio and television away from other communicators, and that therefore candidates should be allowed only so much space or time. To show the irrelevance of this argument, Clagett pointed out that the total cost of all campaigns in 1968 was 16 percent less than the cost of advertising tobacco products in that same year. The compelling need to reduce campaign expenditures was never demonstrated, certainly not to the point of justifying limitations on freedom of speech and of the press, as the law proposed.

The second argument made for the law was that power of communication among political candidates and contributors should be equalized. This objective was to be achieved by limiting the amount of money any one person could contribute and by limiting the amount that candidates could spend. To accomplish these objectives, neither of which has been demonstrated to be socially desirable, the advocates of the law were willing to encroach on First Amendment rights. In the same spirit it might be argued that no newspaper could give more space to one candidate than another, or that no television or radio station could discriminate, at least as to time. The *New York Times* might, for example, be limited to 100,000 words per presidential candidate per week, and the television news programs to thirty minutes per week.

Equalization might be carried further. Candidates could be limited to so many words, to even out the race between fast talkers and slow talkers. They might be required to wear masks, standardized so that physical appearance would not improperly affect the voters, and possibly be required to use voice changers, so that all candidates would sound alike.

In the course of Clagett's presentation, Judge McGowan interrupted with a question as to whether it made a difference "that the newspaper is not going to be elected to office," implying, it seemed, that the First Amendment guarantees did not include candidates for public office. It was not a surprising question in view of the fact that the press generally was supporting the legislation that limited freedom of speech and of communication for others, but not for the press.

The third argument of the reformers was that there was a need to free the political system from corruption. Our lawyers made two arguments against this proposition. First was that the corruption traceable to the methods by which money has been raised for political campaigns in America and to large expenditures was small, marginal, and irrelevant, and that most of the corruption of record would not have been prevented if the statute under test had been on the books. There is little evidence that in politics, money is the root of all evil, as Common Cause proclaims. There is much more evidence that the more corrupting forces are the desires for power and for recognition—traditionally known as "pride."

Watergate, for example, was not caused by large contributors who influenced President Nixon and his administration, nor did it involve large expenditures. It was a petty-cash operation that could just as easily have been carried out had the new Federal Election Campaign Act been in effect.

Nearly everything that the defendants of the election reform law called corruption was illegal before the Federal Election Campaign Act existed. These included such things as burglary, wiretapping, obstruction of justice, corporate campaign contributions, and so forth. The record does show that some large contributors seek and receive special favors. The evidence of corruption most often cited is what is called the "purchase of ambassadorships." It may be questionable practice to award ambassadorships to large contributors, but the record does not show that foreign policy has been corrupted over the years because of this practice. On the contrary, it shows that many large contributors subsequently appointed as ambassadors have served the country well and with good results.

Moreover, there is evidence that large contributors have been highly important in supporting controversial issues and in challenging established ideas, practices, and institutions. The American Revolution, for example, was not financed by small contributions, or with matching funds given by George III. It was financed at critical times by large contributions and loans from persons like Haym Salomon, John Hancock, and others, and by contributions from foreigners like the Marquis de Lafayette, whose help would be illegal under existing law.

Some of the questions asked by the judges suggested that they should have been social psychologists or historical philosophers, rather than lawyers and judges. Judge McGowan asked Mr. Clagett, "Is there no public interest in intellectual corruption that may come about, at least as a candidate views himself, because he has to spend a very large part of his time soliciting contributions in order to pay his expenses, instead of devoting himself to the issues?"

Determining one's own intellectual corruption "as a candidate views himself" scarcely lends itself to legislative determination. The judge, by asking the question, seemed to suggest that it could be determined, and that the Federal Election Campaign Act, if it stood the test of the courts, would free the candidates from this kind of corruption by insulating them more sharply from citizen influence. The McGowan question also reflected a growing, commonly accepted, uncritical opinion that what is needed in public office is someone who is "his own man."

This Platonic concept of pure guardians runs clearly counter to the conception of representative government, which involves some degree of dependency. President Nixon in the Watergate proceedings became "his own man," above the law and beyond accountability, he seemed to believe. Adolf Hitler, too, reached the status of being "his own man."

In any case, the purpose of freeing a candidate from possible "intellectual corruption" or "erosion of spirit" would not justify limiting his freedom of expression or that of his opponents or critics. One might well argue, if one accepted the implication of the McGowan question, that incumbents, Presidents for example, are disturbed, are possibly agitated, are made to feel insecure, even suffer "erosion of spirit," because of press criticism, and that to save them from such effects, press criticism should be limited in amount or to special editions. Cartoons might be banned altogether.

Judge Leventhal asked a question of even greater subtlety. He suggested that money spent above and beyond a certain level had no impact on the outcome of elections, and that spending could reach a point of "marginal efficiency." Beyond that point further expenditures were wasted. Therefore, a ceiling could be imposed without interfering with freedom of communication. (The judge did not go so far as to suggest that additional expenditures above the critical point could be counterproductive and actually interfere with full communication.) The difficulty with the judge's idea is how to determine when the point of marginal efficiency is reached and how to decide who makes that determination.

The judge moved the inquiry to even more remote levels of motivation and behavior when he suggested that if there were a ceiling on what could be collected and spent, candidates could be much more selective among prospective donors, and under less pressure to accept illegal contributions or contributions from questionable sources. The implication of the judge's questions was that they could be answered and that limitations on speech and communication would be justified.

When Judge McGowan asked whether, in the opinion of our lawyers, it might be advisable to limit presidential campaigns to four weeks, and whether such a limitation would be constitutional, we began to wonder what kind of court we were appearing before, for we had thought that our case on First Amendment grounds was so clear as scarcely to need exposition. Yet here were two judges talking about the "marginal efficiency" of communication and suggesting that if ceilings were placed on campaign expenditures, and candidates could turn down bad money or contaminated money and spend only good money, communications would be improved.

The exchanges between the judges and the lawyers were comparable to those between members of the Foreign Relations Committee of the Senate and a group of psychiatrists who, during the Vietnam War, were asked to speak to the committee on the causes of violence, war, and so forth. The psychiatrists persisted in talking politics, while the committee members kept asking psychological and psychiatric questions.

In these court proceedings, while our attorneys sought to keep the court's attention on the constitutional issue, some judges seemed more interested in pursuing their own theories of the causes and effects of political rhetoric, of how much of a candidate's time is spent in raising money, and of what the relationship is between the size of a contribution and the amount of time the candidate (as a candidate or as an elected official) spends listening to the contributor.

The largest contributor to my 1968 campaign gave $500,000. For that I spent an hour and a half talking with him. I do not know how much time I would have spent with the same contributor had I been elected President, but I am sure that the amount of time would have been based on his professional knowledge and competence, rather than on the size of his contribution. In any case, I am sure that to have raised $500,000 in gifts of $1,000 apiece (as the law now limits contributions) from 500 separate contributors would have taken more than an hour and a half of campaign time.

The defendants tried hard to answer the arguments of Mr. Clagett and to justify the limitations on campaign contributions. Lloyd Cutler was hard pressed by Judge Bazelon to explain why a candidate's expenditure should be limited while a newspaper, possibly one opposing the candidate, could print as much as it wished in opposition.

Cutler's strange defense was that "we have made a bet which has been repeated in dozens of opinions on the benefits of a diversified, free, and untrammeled press." He failed to note that we have also, in the First Amendment, made a "bet" on the freedom of speech.

Cutler avoided responding directly to Judge Bazelon's indirect reference to the monopoly character of the press in many communities and went on to say that the press, to a considerable degree, cancels itself out. He did not explain how or where, or give examples. Mr. Cutler should try running in a congressional district, such as Manchester, New Hampshire, and experience the full treatment of the *Manchester Union Leader* before he concludes so easily that the press "cancels itself out."

Cutler cited court decisions sustaining the constitutionality of the Hatch Act, which limits the participation of employees of the federal government in national politics, to justify the limitations on the participation of general citizens in the amendments to the Federal Election Campaign Act. He referred to Justice White's comment on the Hatch Act in which the justice said it was important not only that the government and its employees carry on government according to principles of justice rather than politics, but that they appear to the public to be doing so. Cutler argued that what applies to government employees should also apply to elected officials. This is a new concept of representative government, and logically extended it would lead to establishing a Platonic civil-service government conducted by a designated guardian of proven virtue and intelligence. If the concept were carried further it could be held that anyone not an employee of the federal government should be denied full participation in politics if he or she receives benefits directly or indirectly in a measurable monetary way from the federal government programs.

Full application of this principle could lead to the exclusion from full citizenship of all persons receiving Social Security payments and those anticipating such payments, farmers who are paid subsidies, beneficiaries of Medicaid and Medicare, persons on welfare, and so forth—all on the assumption that money or monetary benefits, even in small amounts and by indirection, tend to corrupt the commonwealth. The principle can be carried past monetary benefits and applied to any benefit that a person might receive from the government, such as education, in consequence of which the beneficiaries' participation in politics might be limited to offset the conditioning effect of the benefits they received.

The second major constitutional point that we sought to make against the legislation was that it violated not only the constitutionally guaranteed right of freedom of speech, but also the constitutionally guaranteed right of freedom of assembly, of which Alexis de Tocqueville said, "The right of association seems to me by nature almost as inalienable as individual liberty."

What was involved in this legislation, as we saw it, was not only a violation of a right of assembly as defined in the Constitution, but of a right preceding the Constitution, in fact the basic justification of the American Revolution: the right of people to organize for political purposes.

Ironically, this major attack on "freedom of assembly" was carried on during the bicentennial year of the signing of the Declaration of Independence. Ralph Winter of the

Yale Law School made the basic case for us in these words:

"We contend that the First Amendment should be read to forbid the establishment of official political parties and candidates, quite as much as it explicitly forbids the establishment of official religions. There can be little doubt that the establishment clause and free exercise clause of the First Amendment are related. Both are designed to maximize the capacity of individuals to follow their consciences. It matters of conscience, faith, and religion, the Constitution clearly dictates that religion is to be free from government control and government is to be free from alliances with religion. When church and state combine, religious freedom is in danger. Similar dangers lurk in the area of political association, political belief, political activity, and political philosophy. Surely the First Amendment protects the free exercise of politics, and had the framers [of the Constitution] faced the possibility of Subtitle H [a section of the tax code] sponsoring political parties, as they faced the reality of official churches, they would have forbidden it."

I think it fair to say that the men who drafted the Constitution never anticipated a time when one or two political parties would be given preferred position—or be legally established. If they had, they undoubtedly would have included one more protection in the Bill of Rights—a provision allowing for the free practice of politics and making unconstitutional any established political party or parties.

It could be just as well argued that television stations are in fact being corrupted, or that there is a possibility that they will be corrupted, through the influence of large advertisers, and that consequently no advertisements costing more than $1,000 per day, per week, or per month or year, could be sold, and that the additional cost of maintaining television be provided by the federal government and limited to the major networks. Other networks would be tolerated, but only if they could make it on limited advertising sales. The same decision might be, too, applied to major newspapers (those that are incorporated), with government subsidies substituted for advertising revenues. It is possible that contributions above a certain level could be denied to universities. Eventually the same rule might be applied to churches, on the assumption that religion is good for the country but churches can be corrupted by large contributors, and hence the two largest denominations should be singled out for government support, while others would be allowed to accept only limited contributions. It could be argued that freedom of religion would, by such action, remain a choice between the top two. The arguments in defense of the federal election law seemed to be that political freedom remained as long as any person could choose between one of the two parties given preferential treatment if he wished to be expedient, or could join or support one or more of the disadvantaged and handicapped parties if he wished to take a longer view.

Our attorney, Ralph Winter, suggested three tests by which the constitutionality of this section of the law might be determined. The first was whether the legislative purpose was primarily nonpartisan and apolitical; second, whether the principal effect of the law would be to limit or further particular political organizations, movements, or candidates; third, whether it would result in excessive governmental entanglement in political parties and/or political activities.

He then argued that the act failed to meet all three of these tests. First, its prime purpose was neither nonpartisan nor apolitical. It did, in fact, finance certain political activities and political organizations that could be clearly identified: it was a law designed by and for the two major political parties, the Democrats and the Republicans, which provided for direct financing of party activities and the candidates of these parties. It was not, he pointed out, "public financing," as it was called, but legislative financing, through an indirect device for setting aside money that would otherwise have gone to meet the general expenses of government. He added, further, that individuals who exercise the checkoff on their income-tax returns first of all do not add a dollar of their own money to the amount they would pay as taxes. Neither do they by that act designate particular parties or candidates as recipients of the dollar checkoff. The effect of their checkoff is to require, under whatever terms for distribution Congress establishes, that one dollar (not the dollar of the taxpayer exercising the checkoff privilege, but a dollar distributed out of the general revenue) will go to the Republican and to the Democratic parties. Whereas the law providing for the checkoff provides for a "yes" or a "no" position, it does not require a majority or even a plurality to activate the program, but rather that each "yes" indication will have the effect of allocating one dollar to the political fund. In recent years, the checkoff has not been supported by the majority of taxpayers, or even by a plurality. The number of anti-checkoff returns has far overrun the positives. In 1977, for example, the IRS returns showed that 28.6 percent checked "yes" as against 45.4 percent who checked "no," with 26 percent taking no position.

If this issue had been offered in a referendum, it would have been rejected. Indications are that the program is likely to become less popular as people come to understand the discriminatory character of the law and realize that the checkoff has the effect of taking their tax money and using it to support parties and candidates whom they may oppose.

It seemed obvious to us that the legislation was discriminatory and partisan and would inevitably involve the government very deeply and extensively in the conduct and control of political activity, and as a consequence, the government would eventually control the very process by which it itself was established and conducted.

The clearest example of this possibility was the provision of the law which allowed an incumbent President, acting through his secretary of the treasury, to exercise discretion in the allocation of available funds among the various candidates eligible for matching grants.

Under the law, the secretary was not required to distribute the money equally, but to "take into account, in seeking to achieve an equitable distribution, the sequence in which such certifications are received." How the sequence bore on equity was not made clear in the law. Clearly, in this case, the government in power could influence an ongoing election by deciding how to distribute limited funds. The Federal Election Commission, whose members were Democrats and Republicans only, also was given powers enabling it to intervene in an election in progress.

When Judge Bazelon pushed Paul J. Mode, Jr., one of the lawyers supporting the legislation, to say why minor parties were any threat to the political system and to orderly elections, and if not, to explain the need to regulate them and discriminate against them, the lawyer did not seem to understand the question and continued to say that the law did not discriminate against them. The fact that major parties would be given some $20 million before starting their campaigns, but minor parties would receive no money in advance and only limited amounts after the election, if they met standards no minor party was likely to meet, did not, in Mr. Mode's mind, constitute discrimination. He suggested that any minor-party candidate could avoid discrimination by running for the nomination of a major party. The judge suggested that if the minor parties were no threat to the public good, and little threat to either the Republican or Democratic party, then there might be no

good reason to limit contributions to them to $1,000. He
also suggested that, because people who contributed to
minor parties might be harassed, perhaps disclosure of
contributors should not be required.

Attorney Joel Gora followed Paul Mode. He addressed
himself principally to the disclosure provisions of the act,
which were of special interest to the New York Civil Liberties Union, for whom he spoke. His special concern
was the provision that applied to nonpartisan groups
whose activities directly or indirectly might affect federal
elections. Gora cited experiences under the disclosure requirements of the 1971 campaign act, when the government went to court in an attempt to shut down a group
called the Committee on Impeachment unless the committee
disclosed the names of its contributors. The government
position was rejected by the court. Gora also cited another
court decision dealing with a legal requirement that any
committee that wanted to join a candidate in a political
stand would have to get prior approval from the candidate
before it mentioned him in an advertisement. The court
held that this requirement of prior approval was an improper restraint.

Gora argued further that organizations that were only
marginally political and were nonpartisan should be exempted from disclosure. He added that the requirement of
disclosure by minority parties was scarcely necessary, since
all minority parties combined spend only about 1 percent
of the political money that is spent in the United States.

Our basic case against disclosure was made on the
issue of privacy and on the practical one of harassment. There is a record of abuse and harassment of members of the Socialist Workers and Communist parties.
The record also shows how minority parties other than
Socialists and Communists could suffer from disclosure;
for example, the Republican party of Mississippi had taken

special precautions by limiting contributions so as to avoid the disclosure requirements of the Mississippi law.

The strongest argument against disclosure is that privacy makes for greater political freedom. In the early history of the country there were some states in which all voting was public. There was no secret ballot. In the name of purer politics in this country and of responsible citizenship, it could be argued that all voting should be public. It is a small step to go from saying that anyone who contributes over $10 to a political effort shall have his or her name and the amount of the contribution on record, to requiring that every vote be openly recorded by public officials and accessible to public scrutiny. Such a requirement would meet one of the arguments for disclosure stressed by Judge Leventhal, namely that without disclosure members of one party could secretly make contributions to a small party, so that it could carry on a campaign that might draw votes away from an opposite major party and thus affect the outcome of the election.

The task of organizing such an effort, by which members of a major party would transfer the needed sums in $10 or even $100 contributions, would require political genius beyond anything yet demonstrated in American politics. The argument for reporting contributions as protection against crossovers is consistent with arguments, now being made in states that do have registration but allow crossovers or that allow independents to vote in primary elections, to tighten state laws so as to limit participation in primaries to established members of the respective parties.

All of these moves run counter to the trend of the last 100 years, which has been to provide more and more privacy in elections. In the state of Minnesota, for example, there is no party designation, and the prospective voter is given a primary ballot that includes the candidates of both parties. He makes his choice of party within the ballot booth.

The third major argument that we made against the law was that the manner in which the Federal Election Commission had been set up was clearly unconstitutional, and more important, even if the FEC were set up according to constitutional rules, the power granted to it clearly involved a violation of the constitutional principle of separation of powers among the executive, the judicial, and the legislative branches of the federal government.

The first point was technical and clearly less important to us than the second. The law, as drafted, provided that the two members of the commission would be appointed by the Senate, two by the House of Representatives, and two by the President. It was conceded by supporters of the legislation that if the functions of the commission were executive, it would be unconstitutional for its members to be appointed by the House and Senate. However, they argued that the commission was an arm of Congress, and therefore its functions were predominantly legislative. At the same time, Common Cause, in one of its briefs, argued that some commission operations, such as the publishing of advisory opinions and holding hearings on violations, were quasi-judicial.

There seemed little question that the commission's principal powers were executive: to police and enforce contribution limits and disclosure provisions of the act and to administer in crucial ways the public-financing provisions of the act. It was also to formulate general policy relative to the administration of the statute, including its criminal provisions. It had been given power to bring civil enforcement actions and to refer criminal violations to the Justice Department. Clearly, under the Constitution, officials with such power had to be nominated by the President and confirmed by the Senate. Defenders of the law did not concede this point before the appeals court. Rather, they chose, speaking through Mr. Spritzer, to argue that we did not have

standing in court to raise the issue of unconstitutionality of
the appointment process since, they said, only the attorney
general, acting for the President, could bring proceedings to
challenge the unconstitutionality of the appointive process.
The implication was that if the President wished to give up
constitutional powers, he could do so and no one would
challenge him.

It was the legislative and judicial powers granted to the
commission, and the potential for their abuse, that we
thought were most clearly subject to constitutional challenge.
For example, the commission was given the unusual grant
of power to direct the attorney general to institute civil
proceedings, including those for civil injunctions, and the
attorney general was required, without any exercise of discretion as prosecutor, to follow the commission order. The
commission had the equivalent of both judicial and legislative power in its authority to grant waivers and exceptions
from its orders. It could, for example, remove the $2 million
limitation on the money allowed the two major parties to
conduct their conventions, by determining that extraordi-
nary and unforeseen circumstances, wholly undefined in the
statute, existed.

The commission was also given the power to disqualify
candidates from holding federal office for as long as six
years. Under the Constitution, Congress is given power to
judge elections, returns, and qualifications of its members.
The power had been treated as a very limited power. In the
case of Congressman Adam Clayton Powell, the Supreme
Court held that congressional power was restricted to
judging those qualifications for holding public office which
are stated in the Constitution.

The Constitution provides only that those elected to the
House and the Senate be citizens of the United States
and residents of the states that elect them. House members
must be twenty-five years old before they can be sworn in,

and senators must be at least thirty years old. In the case of the President, in addition to an age requirement of thirty-five years, there is a requirement that he be born in the United States. Under the Court decision, the House of Representatives could discipline Congressman Powell by taking away special functions given him by the House, but it could not take from him the right to vote in the House or to speak for his constituents.

In cases arising from violations of the old Corrupt Practices Act, which applied to election processes rather than to conduct in office, it had been held that Congress could not refuse to seat a member, although it could subsequently expel him by a two-thirds vote. As Powell's case involved conduct in office, and he had not violated the constitutional qualifications for holding office, the Court held that the House could not refuse to seat him.

A further point of confusion of powers was noted by a Justice Department brief that pointed out that the commission itself had the option of civil enforcement and did not have to refer all such matters to the attorney general, as it did those of a criminal nature. Judge McGowan, who later was to support the law in its entirety while acknowledging the point made by the attorney general, suggested that perhaps it could be overlooked until the commission acted. The commission might, he said, opt always "to refer civil matters to the attorney general for enforcement." In other words, he said, it might be all right to leave the questionable language in the law and to take judicial action only if the commission chose to use the questioned authority.

Under Judge McGowan's proposal, any legislative act, no matter how clearly unconstitutional, might be allowed to stand until an attempt was made to use it. Attorney Ralph Spritzer, later in his presentation, supported the same approach to the testing of a law. While acknowledging that provisions of the statute relating to the disqualification of candidates raised significant constitutional questions, he still proposed that the court wait until the Federal Election Commission had moved to disqualify a candidate. That is, he argued that unconstitutional language be allowed to stand and that its application be dealt with case by case.

The implication of this suggestion is that the Federal Election Commission could disqualify a series of candidates, and the court could declare each disqualification unconstitutional—a strange suggestion to make to a court already overburdened with cases.

The majority of the circuit court supported the legislation. Its opinion was stated in a text of nearly 100 pages, published August 15, 1975, accompanied by some 25 pages of dissenting opinions.

The majority opinion was credited to no one of the subscribing judges. It approved all major provisions of the act. Most of the justifications supporting the decision were sociological, psychological, and philosophical in nature, rather than legal. For example, in concluding its opinion, the majority said, "Our democracy has moved a long way from the town hall, one man, one vote conception of the framers. Politics has become a growth industry and a way of life for millions of Americans." (This latter statement scarcely stands the test of historical examination, unless the number of persons employed by the government and the numbers that may be stirred to action during the campaigns are to be counted. Indifference and disregard of politics by millions, rather than involvement in it as a growth industry, is the more serious problem in America today.)

The majority of the court went on to say that "the corrosive influence of money blights our democratic processes." (The statement had clearly not been demonstrated before the court, but even if it had been proved it would not have been sufficient grounds for overriding constitutionally guaranteed freedoms.) The court continued, in a fine flight of political rhetoric, "We have not been sufficiently vigilant; we have failed to remind ourselves, as we moved from the town halls to today's quadrennial Romanesque political extravagances, that politics is neither an end in itself nor a means for subverting the will of the people." What bearing that great observation had on the court's decision is difficult to comprehend.

The next passage might well have been written, not by the judges but by Common Cause: "The excesses revealed by this record—the campaign spending, the use to which the money is put in some instances, the campaign funding, the quid pro quo for the contributions—support the legislative judgment that the situation not only must not be allowed to deteriorate further, but that the present situation cannot be tolerated by a government that professes to be a democracy. . . . What the Congress has prescribed, and the President has approved, may well be not enough. Lesser measures, taken since 1910, have failed. But these efforts on the part of our government to cleanse its democratic processes should at least be given a chance to prove themselves. Certainly they should not be rejected because they might have some incidental, not clearly defined, effect on First Amendment freedoms." (We clearly had not gotten across the point that the effects were not incidental, but direct, and that they were well defined.)

The majority concluded with a literary reference which is not clear to me. To reject a law that might have incidental First Amendment effects, the court said, "might be Aesopian in the sense of the dog losing his bone going after its deceptively larger reflection in the water."

After adding a number of appendices, the majority of the court, in comments just preceding the dissents, observed that "we have arrived at the comprehensiveness of the present acts through the failure of piecemeal legislation to preserve the integrity of federal elections." Evidently the court believes that the whole is greater than the sum of its parts.

The general position expressed by the majority of the court on most controversial points was that as none of the plaintiffs had as yet been hurt by the law, there was little point in making any constitutional judgments about the text. Fortunately this view was not shared by all the members of the circuit court, nor was it accepted by the Supreme Court.

There were three separate dissents by members of the circuit court. Judge Bazelon took issue with the majority position that the disclosure requirements as applied to minor parties were constitutional. He argued principally from the constitutional guarantee of privacy concerning one's associations and beliefs. Citing previous court decisions, he noted that privacy is safeguarded "first for its own sake, as a fundamental value of any society that respects the dignity of the individual," and is also protected "as a means of achieving the 'uninhibited, robust, and wide-open' debate to which the First Amendment commits us."

"Associational privacy," he noted, "is of particular importance to minor parties. Members of mainstream organizations such as the major parties have little to fear from being so identified. But to be publicly labeled, e.g., Socialist, Communist, or Nazi is to invite social ostracism, loss of business or employment, verbal or physical abuse, or worse." He might have added that the same is true of parties near the mainstream if it can be charged that support of them is likely to draw votes away from one or both of the major parties. He might have cited the workers in company towns in the twenties who were threatened with the closing of mines or factories where they worked if they voted anything but Republican.

His most pointed comment was in response to the court

majority's holding that injury had not been demonstrated. "In the end," he wrote, "the court requires minor parties to prove what is obvious but unprovable, while permitting the government to hypothesize interests which are little more than plausible. This approach stands First Amendment jurisprudence on its head. To justify infringing freedom of speech, a danger must be 'present,' or 'imminent,' not hypothetical. The crucial issues at stake in this case call for strengthening, not relaxing, that requirement."

Judge MacKinnon, in a separate dissent, took particular issue with the court's approval of the Federal Election Commission. "It is my conclusion," he wrote, "that as its membership is presently constituted, it violates the separation of powers of the three branches of government as prescribed by the Constitution."

A third dissenting opinion was submitted by Judge Tamm with Judge Wilkey concurring. Judge Tamm found no constitutional fault with the requirement of disclosure of political contributions to political parties, but felt that the requirement that groups which were marginally political, such as the Civil Liberties Union, publicize their contributors' names was a violation of the constitutionally guaranteed right of privacy.

Tamm and Wilkey concluded that both the limitations on contributions and the limitations on expenditures provided in the statute violated freedom of speech. They especially challenged a line that had been used by defendants in the case, a line based on a case in which the Supreme Court had upheld regulation of sound trucks. Judge Tamm noted that "dollars are *not* merely the functional equivalent of decibels. By regulating sound trucks through a noise ordinance," he noted, "the government was not regulating the *quantity* of speech. . . ."

Judge Tamm also found the public financing provisions of the act defective, observing that since the method pro-

vided for public funding in the act was not the best available
to preserve First Amendment values, it should be set aside.
He added that he thought the act also violated the Fifth
Amendment by denying to minority parties any share of
public money at "a meaningful time."

In addition, he agreed with our position that the manner
in which the Federal Election Commission was established
and the manner in which it was authorized to operate violated the constitutional provisions for the separation of
powers.

By way of concession to the majority members of the
court, he credited them with good intentions such as, he
said, had moved Congress, but then added, "I am afraid
that this phenomenon, coupled with the recognition that we
serve here primarily as the jurisdictional prerequisite to
ultimate Supreme Court disposition, may have partially
contributed to the result reached today."

Federal Election Control, Phase Three

Although we were disappointed by the decision of the appeals court, we were not wholly surprised. The makeup of the court and its anticipation of a Supreme Court review helped to explain the appeals court decision and its majority opinion.

Comparing the majority opinion with the principal minority opinion, we were encouraged by the weakness of the former and its irrelevance insofar as the basic constitutional issues of the case were involved, and by the fact that the record in recent years showed that the Supreme Court had not hesitated to reverse and modify decisions of the appeals court.

One lawyer, after reading the majority opinion of the appeals court, remarked that the biggest burden the lawyers for the defendants of the Federal Election Campaign Act would carry before the Supreme Court would be that of defending the majority opinion of the lower court.

On the other hand, the dissenting opinion of Judge Tamm and Judge Wilkey, as well as the separate dissents of Judge Bazelon and Judge MacKinnon, had avoided sociology, social psychology, and philosophy of history and had stayed close to constitutional issues.

In the briefs submitted before the case was heard by the Supreme Court, the following provisions of the Constitution were noted for the Court's judgment of the case:

Article I, Section 4

"The times, places and manner of holding elections for Senators and Representatives, shall be prescribed in each State by the Legislature thereof: but the Congress may at any time by law make or alter such regulations, except as to the places of choosing Senators."

This article and its application to the Federal Election Campaign Act was of special interest to Senator James Buckley of New York, who had been elected as a third-party candidate before the amendments to the election law were passed and who saw their enactment as a serious threat to any third-party effort in the future. In the debate before the amendments were passed, he labeled them the "Incumbent Protection Act of 1974," one that would protect incumbent members of Congress, both Democrats and Republicans, as well as the interests of the two established parties, against future third-party challenges.

Article I, Section 8, Clause 1

This is the general welfare clause of the Constitution which, in short, states that the Congress shall have power to provide for the general welfare of the United States. Much of the argument of the defendants of the election law was based on a vague appeal that the bill was necessary to serve the "general welfare."

Article II, Section 2, Clause 2

This article states, "He [the President] shall nominate, and by and with the advice and consent of the Senate, shall appoint ambassadors, other public ministers and consuls, judges of the Supreme Court, and all other officers of the United States, whose appointments are not herein otherwise provided for, and which shall be established by law: but the Congress may by law vest the appointment of such inferior officers, as they think proper, in the President alone, in the courts of law, or in the heads of departments."

This section of the Constitution bore on the question of whether the methods of appointing the members of the Federal Election Commission, as specified by the new law, were constitutional or not. Our lawyers argued that the procedure was clearly unconstitutional. The defending lawyers argued that it was constitutional.

Amendment I

"Congress shall make no law respecting an establishment of religion, or prohibiting the free exercise thereof; or abridging the freedom of speech, or of the press; or the right of the people peaceably to assemble, and to petition the Government for a redress of grievances."

This, the First Amendment to the Constitution, we considered central to our case. We saw the election law as encroaching on the freedom of speech and of the press, and severely limiting the right of people to assemble, i.e., to organize for political purposes, which in a democratic political system is the fundamental act of petition.

Amendment IV

"The right of the people to be secure in their persons, houses, papers, and effects, against unreasonable searches and seizures, shall not be violated, and no warrants shall issue, but upon probable cause, supported by oath or affirmation, and particularly describing the place to be searched, and the persons or things to be seized."

This provision of the Constitution was emphasized by the lawyers for the New York Civil Liberties Union, as it had been in the dissenting opinion of Judge Bazelon, as being especially important to minority and ideological parties such as the Socialists and the Communists.

Amendment V

"No person shall be . . . deprived of life, liberty, or property, without due process of law."

We thought the Fifth Amendment was involved in some of the more technical constitutional issues of the election statute: the ones that bore on eligibility for office, the denial of the right to run for office, the authority given the Federal Election Commission, and other fine points of constitutional law.

Amendment IX

"The enumeration in the Constitution, of certain rights, shall not be construed to deny or disparage others retained by the people."

We suggested that the election act denied or disparaged rights retained by the people.

On November 14, 1975, oral arguments were heard by the Supreme Court. Justice William O. Douglas missed part of the hearing because he was suffering from an illness which subsequently brought about his resignation from the Court. The other justices heard all the arguments.

Our spokesmen made essentially the same arguments before the Supreme Court that they had before the circuit court. Ralph Winter led off in presenting the argument that limitations on both campaign expenditures and campaign contributions inhibited freedom of speech and freedom of assembly, and also gave special advantages to incumbent officeholders. He cited campaigns that would have been seriously handicapped if the law under review had been in effect, such as the anti-war campaign of 1968, the Buckley Senate campaign in 1970, and the McGovern presidential campaign of 1972.

Winter concluded his presentation with this statement: "The greatest campaign reform law ever enacted was the

First Amendment: we rely on the proposition that good speech will drive out bad, and all appellants ask is that the Court enforce that."

The most persistent questioner on the issue of the effect of the legislation on freedom of speech was Justice Potter Stewart. Joel Gora of the New York Civil Liberties Union argued the case against disclosure of names of contributors, not on the grounds that disclosure was inherently unconstitutional, but on the grounds that the regulation went far beyond reasonable provisions for disclosure, concerning both the threshold and the range of activities for which reporting of contributions was required. He pointed out that the law, as drafted, provided that any citizen who, on his own, spent more than $100 on federal politics in any one year and did not identify himself with a particular candidate or campaign—someone who, for example, printed a pamphlet or bought an advertisement attacking the position of a member of Congress—was required to register and file reports with the Federal Election Commission, and that the penalty for noncompliance with the disclosure and filing requirements was one year in jail and a $1,000 fine.

The Court seemed surprised.

Gora then asked the Court to consider three possible remedies: one, raising the amount at which reporting was required; two, exempting from disclosure requirements citizens' efforts that were independent of political campaigns; and three, exempting minority parties from requirements.

The Justice Department sent up attorney Daniel Friedman, deputy solicitor general, as its principal voice in support of the legislation. A Justice Department that understood its function in the United States government might have sent someone to speak on the constitutional issues involved, and possibly to address the problems and the methods of administration affecting the Justice Depart-

ment. Friedman did neither of these things, but largely
defended the purpose of the legislation. He said that "by
the early 1970s there was a tremendous feeling in this
country that you couldn't trust the government; a lack of
electorate confidence in our government officials; the no-
tion that somehow people could be bought if you gave
enough money." He produced no evidence from Justice
Department studies or investigations to prove any of these
assertions, nor did he cite nongovernmental polls or studies.

Friedman seemed to think that a strong argument for
the law was that its disclosure provisions would expose persons who contributed to competing candidates, as though
this were a basic corruption of the political system. He
continued, "Those people are obviously hopeful that . . ."
and it was clear that he meant to go on to say that they
were hopeful of buying influence or goodwill. He was interrupted by the chief justice, who asked him to explain motivations of a person who, for example, "would put up half
a million dollars or a million, whatever it takes, for a series
of three national television debates between two candidates,
or within a state, if it's a senatorial race. . . . Now," continued the justice, "he's contributing to both sides, isn't he,
when he finances that? Anything improper in that?" The
spokesman for the Justice Department had no clear answer
to the chief justice's question.

One of the justices asked a question affecting the broad
policy of election financing.

"As I understand it, corporations and unions," the justice said, "are exempted from the spending and contribution requirements of this act. . . . And the union [or] the
corporation, as the case may be, has the authority under 610
[a section of the act] to organize that fund, and they solicit
the money for the fund from stockholders, employees and
union members. Now you're talking about the corrosive
or corroding effect of large concentrations of wealth. How

do you explain the exemption of corporations and unions from this act?"

What follows is part of Mr. Friedman's response. "There are problems. I think there is a problem. . . . that is an issue that initially, I suppose, the Federal Election Commission will have to resolve."

When the Justice Department lawyer tried to return to the disclosure issue, a justice said, "Mr. Friedman, I don't want to deter you from proceeding, but I would like to invite your attention to the statement in the brief filed by the attorney general as *amicus*. On page 74 the brief says flatly that corporations and unions can accept and spend funds without limit, supporting or advocating the defeat of candidates. Now, of course, the brief could be wrong, as I think you suggest, but I wanted to call that to your attention."

Friedman responded, "Well, a footnote in another brief that I cannot locate at the moment takes issue with it." Subsequently, Friedman, in his nonjudicial defense of the act, cited a case in which a senator had, in a single day of a campaign, received 247 contributions totaling $28,025 from individuals, all employees of a single corporation.

A justice responded by saying, "And yet, Mr. Friedman, could that corporation have set up a segregated fund and solicited or set up a desk in the front office and said that anyone that wants to can contribute, and 247 came along, made contributions totaling $28,025; and then under the attorney general's suggestion, I gather that could have been spent by that fund any way they wanted, without any disclosure of the names of those 247."

The Justice Department had no clear answer. Finally the Court put the hard issue to Friedman, which was, "It's a First Amendment problem." Friedman answered, "Yes." The justice then followed by saying, "That any First Amendment rights are overridden by compelling governmental interests. That's your basic argument, isn't it?" Friedman answered, "That's our basic argument. If I may rephrase it slightly, any adverse impact upon First Amendment rights is overridden by the compelling government interests." (Most of this questioning was conducted by Justices William Brennan and Potter Stewart.)

Finally, Friedman was reminded that he had referred to the "most fundamental of all our rights: the right to vote." The justice asked, "Is it your position that the United States Constitution places the right to vote in a position superior to the right to speak or publish?" Mr. Friedman replied in the negative. And so on that note the Justice Department, having advocated a limitation of freedom of speech as necessary to prevent an unproved contention of corruption of the electoral process, ended its argument.

Mr. Friedman was followed by Archibald Cox, formerly a special prosecutor in the Justice Department, who was prepared to defend the spending and contribution limits in the law. He represented, as friends of the court, Senators Hugh Scott and Edward Kennedy. The Cox presentation never took any clear form, as the justices interrupted frequently, asking him to supply constitutional, legal, or historical justification for his arguments.

The concluding presentation for those opposing the legislation was made by Brice Clagett, who concentrated especially on the effect of the law on presidential elections and third-party activities.

First Clagett argued that the act was obviously discriminatory in that it provided approximately $20 million to the two established major parties in advance of the presidential campaign, while denying any advance money to new parties. Second, he pointed out the provision of the law by which new parties could get a pro-rata, post-election funding if they received 5 percent or more of the vote, and declared it faulty on two counts; the 5 percent require-

ment was too high, and the potential entitlement after the
5 percent vote had been achieved was further limited to the
payment of outstanding loans. There were two effects of
these provisions of the law: first, to leave the new party
without any assurance or certainty of post-election funding;
and second, since such parties could receive nothing beyond money to settle outstanding obligations, they would
have no financial base upon which to build for the next
election. They would be thrown back to a zero position,
whereas the major parties could anticipate $20 million or
more in advance of the next presidential election. Obviously, it was a political Catch-22 situation.

Mr. Lloyd Cutler, who followed Mr. Clagett, opened his
statement on behalf of the Center for Public Financing of
Elections and the League of Women Voters by suggesting
that some of the plaintiffs had no standing on the issue of
public financing because they lacked an interest in the
public financing of presidential campaigns. It was a curious
argument to make in a case that hung on basic constitutional issues in which every citizen had an interest.

Clagett, in his rebuttal, raised the issue of the constitutionality of having general revenue allocated to the financing of specific political party activities and cited in
support of his argument a Supreme Court decision in *International Machinists Association* v. *Street*. In that case the
Court held that the First Amendment was violated when
union dues were used to support political candidates with
whom some members disagreed. Clagett, in his concluding
statement, pointed out that even though a system for financing federal elections that was less discriminatory than
the one being proposed could be designed, any such system
would be unconstitutional. It would involve the government, i.e., the state, in political activity.

Clagett then argued that the Federal Election Commission had been established unconstitutionally, and further,

even though the commission might be set up by constitutional procedures, the powers given to it by the law, powers
that it had begun to exercise, were unconstitutional, as they
violated in the most serious way the constitutional principle
of the separation of powers.

The strength of Clagett's argument is demonstrated by
this exchange among him and Justice Rehnquist and other
members of the Court.

> *Justice Rehnquist:* ". . . you say it *is* a legislative
> agency."
> *Clagett:* "Yes, sir."
> *Justice:* "Because of its membership, because of who
> appointed a majority of its membership, or because
> of its functions?"
> *Clagett:* "Who appoints the membership."
> *Justice:* "Which?"
> *Clagett:* "Who appoints the membership, plus the
> legislative veto. . . ."

And a second exchange:

> *Justice:* "Suppose all the members were presidential
> appointees, but either house could veto, as it is
> now?"
> *Clagett:* "We think it would then be an executive
> agency; but the legislative veto would be bad."
> *Justice:* "So that just the legislative veto itself renders
> the scheme unconstitutional?"
> *Clagett:* "Yes. Oh, yes, we think so, Your Honor."

And a third exchange:

> *Justice:* "How would you classify the power to strike
> a candidate from the ballot; in which of the three
> categories would you say that falls [i.e., would this
> power put the election commission in the legislative,
> executive, or judicial category]?"
> *Clagett:* "I would have to put that in a fourth category,

Mr. Chief Justice, and say that it's something that no one can do, whether the executive, the legislative, or the judiciary. . . ."

Justice: "You don't think the judicial review saves it any, if the initial power rests with the commission?"

Clagett: "No, I don't think that saves it at all, Mr. Chief Justice. It seems to me to be a power on which the constitutional convention is quite clear. It should not be exercised by anyone. All the comments of the Framers, which are set out at such great length in *Powell* v. *McCormack,* to the effect that it must be the people who choose their representatives, and that if there are to be any limitations on who can become representatives, it must be the Constitution itself which imposes them, and no others. No others can sneak in there in any way whatsoever."

Mr. Spritzer, coming on after Clagett, raised again the issue of the standing of some of the plaintiffs which had been raised earlier by Mr. Cutler. A justice responded in these words: "Well, since this commission is doing something to restrict any one of these plaintiffs, then surely the plaintiffs have standing to attack the constitutional validity of the commission. And it's not—they're not being champions of the President. They're being champions, self-appointed if you will, of the Constitution."

The confusion concerning the powers granted to the commission by the statute was clearly demonstrated in this exchange between the Court and Mr. Spritzer.

The Court: ". . . you must, then, assert and claim that Congress could itself, through its own agency, through some of its committees, do all the investigation necessary to recommend to the attorney general that a criminal prosecution be pursued?"

Mr. Spritzer: "Yes. And Congress did many of these things under the 1910 Act, under the 1925 Act,

through the Secretary of the Senate and the Clerk
of the House."

The Court: "They could have their own Federal Bureau of Investigation to carry things out, and present them to the attorney general?"

Mr. Spritzer: "Well, they certainly . . ."

The Court: "Under Title 18, under any of the Title 18
provisions . . . ?"

And so the case ran down, and at 3:33 P.M. on November 10, 1975, the case was submitted. The Supreme Court
issued its decision on January 30, 1976.

The Court held that the $1,000 limitation on contribu-
tions by individuals to candidates and authorized campaign
committees was constitutional, largely on the ground that
such limitations would prevent corruption or the appearance of corruption in the political process. It also approved
the $5,000 limitation on contributions by political commit-
tees and the $25,000 limitation on an individual's total
contributions in any calendar year.

However, the Court found the $1,000 limitation on ex-
penditures on behalf of a particular candidate by an individual acting independently of a campaign or of a candidate to be clearly unconstitutional. The majority of the
Court noted that the plain effect of this provision of the law
was "to prohibit all individuals, who are neither candidates
nor owners of institutional press facilities, and all groups,
except political parties and campaign organizations, from
voicing their views. . . ." The provision would, as the
Court noted, have made it a federal criminal offense for a
person or association of persons to place a single one-
quarter-page advertisement "relative to a clearly identified
candidate" in a major metropolitan newspaper.

The Court also noted that the argument for the limitation
on independent expenditures as necessary to prevent corruption of the political system had little to support it, and

also totally rejected the claim that such a limitation would serve to equalize the influence of persons on the political process. The idea, the Court wrote, "that government may restrict the speech of some elements of our society in order to enhance the relative voice of others is wholly foreign to the First Amendment. . . ." The Court noted further that "protection against governmental abridgment of free expression cannot properly be made to depend on a person's financial ability to engage in public discussion."

The Court then took up the matter of the limitations on expenditures by candidates using personal and family resources. The Court held these restrictions to be unconstitutional interferences with the First Amendment guarantees of individual freedom of speech and also declared that the overall limitations on expenditures in campaigns for the House of Representatives, the Senate, and the presidency were also unconstitutional.

The media, in their reports of this decision, generally ignored its emphasis on protecting and defining freedom of speech and of the press and instead said the Court had "protected the fat cats."

The Supreme Court upheld the disclosure provisions of the act, saying that a record of harassment and of chilling effect had not been shown, and further, that if such a record were presented, "We [the Court] cannot assume that courts will be insensitive to similar showings [such as those made in a case involving disclosure of contributors to the NAACP] when made in future cases."

The Court rejected our basic argument that the provisions of the law that gave advance funding to the Republican and the Democratic parties, and included a highly questionable formula by which other parties might receive funding after the election was over, and then only to meet accumulated debts, were unconstitutional. In a footnote to the opinion, the Court made the observation that "since the public financing provisions have never been in operation, appellants are unable to offer factual proof that the scheme is discriminatory in its effect. In rejecting appellants' arguments, we of course do not rule out the possibility of concluding in some future case, upon an appropriate factual demonstration, that the public financing system invidiously discriminates against non-major parties."

It was the Court's opinion on this section that we thought failed most seriously to perceive the basic unconstitutionality of a law which, in effect, established two political parties with special privileges and advantages. The Court observed that our citing of the constitutional ban against supporting one or more religions was not an acceptable analogy.

After summarizing the powers given to the Federal Election Commission by the act, the Court examined the question of the way the commission members were appointed, and therefore whether the commission could constitutionally exercise the powers conferred upon it. The Circuit Court of Appeals had held that it could, calling our arguments "strikingly syllogistic," whatever that means.

The Supreme Court, in commenting on the appeals court's words and actions, said, "We do not think appellants' arguments . . . may be so easily dismissed as did the majority of the Court of Appeals." The Supreme Court cited Madison's argument in the *Federalist* No. 47, which gave Montesquieu's grounds for the separation of powers in a democratic government. "When the legislative and executive powers are united in the same person or body," Montesquieu had written, "there can be no liberty, because apprehensions may arise lest the same monarch, or senate, should enact tyrannical laws to execute them in a 'tyrannical manner,' " and added, "Were the power of judging joined with the legislative, the life and liberty of the subject would be exposed to arbitrary control, for the judge would then be the legislator. Were it joined to the executive power, the judge might behave with all the violence of an oppressor."

On the basis of this fundamental interpretation of the separation-of-powers provision of the Constitution, sustained by court decisions, the Supreme Court held that the election commission had been established by an unconstitutional process. The commission was given a life of thirty days during which it might carry on its duties, after which, unless it had been reappointed and reestablished in conformity with the Constitution, it would cease to exercise its most important powers.

Five of the eight justices who heard the case filed opinions dissenting in part from the majority opinion. The most comprehensive and far-reaching dissent was that of Chief Justice Warren Burger.

Burger first dissented from the majority's holding that sustained the provisions requiring disclosure of small contributions to candidates and to campaign committees. He argued principally against the low level of the disclosure requirements, asserting that the public purpose of avoiding corruption or the appearance of corruption was not served by such low threshold limits, and that the public had no right to know about private political contributions in the amount of $100 plus $1. He further noted that "no legitimate public interest has been shown in forcing the disclosure of modest contributions that are the prime support of new, unpopular, or unfashionable political causes."

Approving what the Court had done in removing the limits on campaign expenditures, the chief justice questioned its approval of the limits on contributions. He challenged the distinction that the Court had attempted to make between an individual's expenditure on his own communication and his contribution for communications made by another person, committee, or organization. It was a proper question for the chief justice to raise, for the limitations as approved by the majority of the Court impinged both on freedom of speech and on freedom of association, and was scarcely different from saying that a person has full freedom of speech and of the press only if he speaks alone, or sets his own type, or writes his own speeches, but that his freedom is limited if he speaks in chorus, or through some other person or agency. The limits on contributions, the chief justice said, "will, in specific instances, limit exactly the same political activity that the expenditure ceilings limit."

He further challenged the Court's attempt to distinguish "the communication inherent in political *contributions* from the speech aspects of political *expenditures*." This is a distinction which, he said, "simply will not wash." He pointed out what he saw as another contradiction in the Court's decision, which was that the Court, in approving the contribution limits, must "accept the proposition that 'pooling' money is fundamentally different from other forms of associational or joint activity."

Burger rejected as unconstitutional the whole idea of having the government fund political campaigns, including those provisions of the act that allowed matching funds for candidates who met certain conditions in presidential primaries.

He then observed that since that part of the act which the Court had left standing created many significant inequities, the entire act should be rejected. He said that it was a questionable use of the severability clause "to salvage parts of a comprehensive, integrated statutory scheme which, standing alone, are unworkable and in many aspects unfair."

He then concluded his dissent with these words: "To limit either contributions or expenditures as to churches would plainly restrict 'the free exercise' of religion. In my view Congress can no more ration political expression than it can ration religious expression; and limits on political or religious contributions and expenditures effectively curb expression in both areas. There are many prices we pay for the freedoms secured by the First Amendment; the risk of undue influence is one of them, confirming what we have long known: freedom is hazardous, but some restraints are worse."

And so over the chief justice's and our protests, the political processes of the country were delivered into the hands of a new bureaucracy, the Federal Election Commission.

Federal Election Control, Phase Four: The Bureaucrats Take Over

As James Madison wrote in the *Federalist* No. 47, the combination of legislative, executive, and judicial powers in the same hands "may justly be pronounced the very definition of tyranny." The victims of such abuse of power in the colonies had no constitutional protection, no recourse except appeal to the king or revolt. After enduring injustices and the indignities of magistrate proceedings to the point where they were no longer tolerable, the American colonies revolted against the British government.

Two hundred years after that revolution the Congress of the United States, supported by presidential endorsement, gave to an agency of government, the Federal Election Commission, in the name of political reform, power to make rulings and judgments encroaching on freedom of speech, freedom of assembly, and other constitutional guarantees.

Because the Federal Election Campaign Act is highly complex in many provisions and extremely vague in many others, the power to interpret is the power to make law. Relief, if it comes after an election has been lost, is not very satisfying to the losers. Nor is it good for the stability, confidence, and strength of a political system.

Rulings made by the Federal Election Commission in 1975 and 1976 and later are only being sorted out now, long after the elections to which they applied are matters of history. Among these lawmaking pronouncements were the following: interim guidelines to govern a special New Hampshire election; eligibility of contributions for matching funds under the terms of the act; interim guidelines to govern a special Tennessee election; spending limits applicable to a candidate running for two federal offices at the same time; opinion on attorney's or accountant's fees as expenditures; disclosure regulations; office-account regulations; rules on delegates to national nominating conventions; rules on contributions and expenditures and on contributions to a candidate from members of his immediate family.

The commission as reconstituted following the Supreme Court decision promulgated new regulations. But as an indication of the confusion of its operations, even though rules and regulations were being followed by candidates and campaign committees, none was legally in effect in 1976, because Congress adjourned on October 1, 1976, two legislative days before the new commission's rules would have taken effect.

The case of congressional candidate Edward Koch of New York is indicative of the operations of the Federal Election Commission.

On August 27, 1976, Koch's treasurer asked whether the campaign committee could issue campaign buttons reading "Carter-Mondale-Koch" without making an illegal contribution to the other candidates named on the button.

According to a *New York Times* report on the inquiry, the commission was "deadlocked, almost hopelessly" and delayed a response to Koch's request for weeks. The Koch idea was not unusual or without precedent in American politics. However, it created a very difficult problem for the FEC. Candidate Carter, whose name was to appear on the button, had chosen to accept federal subsidies for his general election campaign. Therefore, according to the federal election law, he could not accept private contributions to his campaign. The question before the commission was whether the inclusion of the names "Carter-Mondale" on Koch's buttons was a contribution to Carter or an independent expenditure by Representative Koch (that is, expenditures made by a person beyond Carter's or Mondale's control and acting without any coordination with their campaigns). The commission, after weeks of deliberation and without explanation, decided that the cost of printing the names would not be counted as a contribution to the presidential election. In a subsequent case involving a congressional candidate who wanted to publish a brochure containing a picture of presidential candidate Carter, the FEC again gave its approval, without explanation. Possibly the FEC thought that the picture in the brochure helped neither the congressional candidate nor the presidential candidate.

Then came the case of Congressman Parren Mitchell of Maryland, who was running for reelection to the House of Representatives. He proposed to buy a newspaper advertisement supporting his candidacy and to include in it pictures of the Democratic presidential and vice-presidential candidates, as well as the Democratic candidate for the Senate in Maryland. The FEC, with complete disregard for its ruling in the earlier cases, ruled that it would be illegal for the Mitchell campaign to pay the entire cost of the proposed advertisement, since "a portion of such a payment would be necessarily regarded as an in-kind contribution to the Carter-Mondale ticket."

In a second area of campaign activity (in this case fundraising), the commission has shown similar inconsistency. Early in Carter's 1976 campaign for the Democratic nomination, a rock group, the Allman Brothers, played at the Carter rallies. The standard procedure was to feature the musicians, after which candidate Carter appeared, said little more than "I'm Jimmy Carter. I'm running for President of the United States," smiled, and left the stage.

The FEC considered receipts from these concerts as bona fide campaign contributions, eligible for matching federal money. The program and the tickets, the FEC held, stated the purpose of the rally clearly enough to meet FEC standards.

But in the case of a Linda Ronstadt concert to benefit Jerry Brown's 1976 campaign, the FEC found that those who attended were not clearly informed that the purpose was to raise money. The FEC ruled that although the money collected could be given to the Brown campaign, no matching government funds would go to Brown.

One interesting point of law at issue in the two cases is that under the federal election laws, persons other than the candidate cannot contribute more than $1,000 to a campaign. Thus, it would seem that if the Ronstadt concert receipts were collected from persons who thought that they were paying to hear Linda sing, the IRS would have to rule that the concert receipts were income to Linda and therefore subject to taxation. If she had already made a $1,000 contribution to the Brown campaign, she could not have contributed further to that campaign.

In a similar case involving the McCarthy campaign, the FEC came up with a ruling that was different from both the Allman Brothers and the Ronstadt rulings. In 1977 the FEC brought court action against the "Committee for a Constitutional Presidency—McCarthy '76." The FEC charged that the committee had violated the Federal Election Campaign Act by reporting certain payments as "other receipts" rather than "contributions."

As shown by reports filed with the FEC during 1974, 1975, and 1976 (all, incidentally, years in which the FEC was operating under questionable constitutional or statutory authority), the sums involved were payments made for speeches given by the candidate, principally before college groups. The speeches had been scheduled by the campaign committee, or in its name by a booking agency, and most were paid for out of student activity funds rather than out of university or college funds.

The law itself and the regulations and published instructions from the FEC about reporting such payments were complex and vague. Early rulings held that honoraria paid to incumbents during campaigns should be treated as campaign contributions, rather than income to the candidate. But the Congress reversed this rule as it applied to candidates who were incumbents on the assumption that such candidates could raise enough campaign money from other sources and therefore preferred to treat income from their speeches as personal income. In its haste to clear up this point, Congress made no reference to how payments made for speeches by nonincumbents should be treated. Our interpretation was consistent with the earlier FEC ruling for both incumbents and nonincumbent candidates.

A substantive issue in this case was that if the payments were treated as income, they were taxable as personal income to the candidate, who could then contribute some or all to the campaign.

The FEC held that if a speech was made before "substantial numbers of people" (it did not give a number) comprising part of the candidate's electorate, the speech presumably was intended to enhance the individual's candidacy and the receipts would be considered a "contribution." The FEC then asserted that if it could be shown that the speech was not a campaign speech or was not for the purpose of enhancing the candidacy, the payment was income to the candidate. In making this argument, the FEC made no reference to what the purposes of the Allman Brothers or Linda Ronstadt concerts might have been.

The district court concluded that while my committee

may have committed a technical violation of the act, in reporting the way it did, nonetheless the FEC was not entitled to relief. It is noteworthy that, by the time the court handed down its decision, the FEC had not published its audit of President Carter's nonprimary campaign financing.

The district court's position reflected the uncertainty of the law and the confusion of the FEC rulings. On March 7, 1979, the court found that the treasurer of our committee had shown good faith and diligence and had followed advice of the Government Accounting Office in reporting payments. The court cited a 1976 amendment to the federal election laws which stated that when treasurers and candidates "show that best efforts have been used to obtain and submit the information required . . . they shall be deemed to be in compliance . . ."

Since some of the actions in dispute occurred before the 1976 amendments to the 1974 law, the case was further complicated, a fact noted by the court in its observance that "a candidate today who had conducted himself like defendant would most likely have committed no violation at all, because of the amendment . . ."

After all of this, Judge Louis Oberdorfer concluded his opinion with these words: "The uncertainty of the law, the unfairness of stigmatizing a candidate and his staff when they acted in good faith, and the absence of injury to the public interest which failure to grant relief would cause plaintiff raise equities which decisively outweigh those equities favoring an order as requested by the FEC. The Court therefore declines to enter such an order, grants defendant's motion for summary judgment."

Examples of the arbitrariness of the FEC rulings and of their contradictory nature are almost as numerous as are the rulings themselves. Three characteristics seem to be emerging as the commission continues its work. One is that incumbents are treated differently, that is, better and with more respect, than the nonincumbent challengers; two, the Republicans and Democrats are treated better, with respect to timely response and rules and regulations, than are independent or other-party candidates or their committees; and three, winners are treated differently from losers. As John R. Bolton notes in an article in the July/August 1978 issue of the magazine *Regulation,* "One consistent theme in commission pronouncements is that whenever the statute offers the option, the commission rules in favor of incumbents. This pattern is based on unhappy experiences of the FEC's childhood, against which it has been guarding ever since. The very first set of regulations it proposed provided for close regulation of, and limitations on, congressional 'office accounts.' The Senate, making use of the legislative veto, promptly torpedoed those proposed regulations. As time passed, the commission made revision after revision to the regulations, in the course of which substantive limitations on the office accounts disappeared. Only disclosure now remains."

The commission has learned its lesson and seems to understand that its survival may well depend upon whether it anticipates congressional criticism, which is likely to become more severe as congressmen have more experience with bureaucratic interference with their campaigns and with the conduct of their offices.

One of the earliest FEC rulings demonstrating its special regard for Republicans and Democrats was the one involving the financing of the presidential debates. In several decisions, over the years, federal courts have held it unconstitutional to apply campaign regulations to nonpartisan, issue-oriented groups. Thus the courts held that the disclosure provisions of the 1971 Federal Election Campaign Act could not be applied to the American Civil Liberties Union. In 1976, the Supreme Court held that the similar disclosure provisions included in the 1974 campaign act could not be applied to similar groups. Nonetheless, the FEC has tried to regulate what the courts have said should not be regulated. In separate rulings involving the Sierra Club and the United States Chamber of Commerce, the FEC applied disclosure requirements to the following activities: the publication and distribution of voting records which indicate that the votes were "correct" or "incorrect"; the publication and distribution of answers to questionnaires; and even the preparation of candidate "profiles" which evaluate performance but which do not explicitly urge election or defeat of the candidate.

A clear example of commission proceedings can be found in its case against the Central Long Island Tax Reform Immediately Committee. This group had published a pamphlet citing the voting record of Representative Jerome Ambro on fiscal legislation. The pamphlet did not recommend political action against Ambro, but urged citizens to communicate with Ambro or his staff and make their views known. The FEC held that there was reason to believe that the committee had violated the law in failing to report the $135 spent on its pamphlet.

In contrast with these actions against nonpolitical groups was the FEC's action on the financing of the 1976 presidential debates under the sponsorship of the League of Women Voters. When the League of Women Voters Education Fund offered to sponsor the series of debates (limited to the Democratic and Republican presidential candidates), the commission issued a policy statement which said that the expenses of the Education Fund would be treated neither as contributions to candidates Ford and Carter, nor as expenditures (independent or otherwise) for the benefit of either candidate. In addition, the FEC ruled that the expenditures need not be publicly reported. All of that suggested that the FEC judged the financing of the debates to be wholly nonpolitical and therefore beyond its jurisdiction. Not so. For the FEC went on to forbid the Education Fund from accepting direct corporate or union contributions to support the debates, while at the same time it permitted contributions in unlimited amounts from individuals as well as from corporate and union political-action committees. The FEC enforced this restriction on direct corporate and union contributions for the debates, although it had allowed such contributions to support earlier debates of candidates for the Democratic party nomination, also sponsored by the League of Women Voters.

The FEC never explained the contradiction between its earlier ruling on the debates between the Democratic candidates and its later ruling on the debates between President Ford and candidate Carter. Nor did it explain why exceptions to the legal limitation on contributions could be made for the support of the candidates of the two parties, to the exclusion of all other candidates, when the limitations would have applied if only one candidate had appeared. If this rule were to be accepted, it would follow that as long as one person or committee makes contributions to two or more candidates (of different parties), there should be no limitation on the total contribution.

The FEC explained its ruling with this sentence: "Unlike sponsorship of an appearance by a single candidate, the unavoidable impact of which is to advance the chances of that candidate's election, the debate described in the League proposal does not involve that kind of advocacy or assistance to a campaign to which the Act's contribution limits are directed."

The fact that the debates were quite certain to advance the interests of at least one and possibly both of the candidates included in them, to the disadvantage of all other candidates, seemed not to bother the FEC.

A more detailed explanation, although not a more convincing one, was given in the September/October 1978 issue of the magazine *Regulation* in an article by John G. Murphy, Jr., who was general counsel to the Federal Election Commisson at the time of the League ruling. "Basically," wrote Murphy, "the commission's policy statement, publicly debated at length before issuance, said that an individual's donation to the fund to defray debate costs would not be deemed to be 'for the purpose of influencing the election of any person to federal office' and could therefore be unlimited, but that a similar donation to the fund by a corporation or union would be 'in connection with' a federal election and was therefore prohibited. This is by no means a result clearly directed by the law (on this issue, there is no result directed by the law) and its conceptual rationale is thin at least in allowing unlimited donations by an individual. But the practical reality of the times left the commission with little choice but to find some funding leeway; there was enormous public desire for the debates to go forward and to many it was unthinkable that the election laws could somehow get in the way of an event of such politically historic (even festive) proportions. I recall the *Washington Star* editorially advising the FEC to 'call off its bureaucratic dogs' in this connection . . ." Murphy argued "enormous public desire" was sufficient reason for a ruling that was not directed by law and that involved contradiction of earlier rulings. How he or the FEC measured the "enormity" of the public desire Murphy does not set forth in his article, nor does he explain why "enormous public desire" (even if that desire has been isolated and measured) demands an affirmative, extralegal, bureaucratic response. Certainly "Murphy's law," or procedure of lawmaking, is a new concept in which a government bureau sensing "public desire" and responding to the "urgings of the press" could, on its own, without regard for statute or court decisions, determine what the law is.

Further evidence of discrimination in favor of incumbents,

both Republican and Democratic, is given in the article by John Bolton in the July/August 1978 issue of *Regulation*. Bolton states that as of the date of his article, the FEC had filed over 100 civil suits against people whom the commission held did not file proper reports. According to Bolton, most of the suits were filed against third-party or independent candidates, or nonincumbent candidates seeking the nomination of one of the two major parties. Among those sued were the Socialist Workers party, the Prohibition party, La Raza Unida, and the Communist party.

Most of the nonfilers being pursued by the commission were innocent persons who had little or no knowledge of the federal election law and who did not understand the law or have the staff to file the multitudinous reports required by the commission.

Some indication of the complexity of the act and the difficulty of complying with it is demonstrated in this letter from Stewart R. Mott, a person experienced in politics and political finances and aided by a competent staff. It was sent to Neil Staebler of the Federal Election Commission.

13 November 78

Hon. Neil O. Staebler

—continuation of 11/4/78 letter—

Dear Neil:

Wow! I just discovered that I'm *really* in deep trouble.

Since writing to you on 11/4, I came across two additional violations of the FECA which are substantial, and I might as well mention two others that are minor. You'll remember that my 10/6/78 report totaled $24,950. Well, one candidate, Max Heller, sent back his $100 saying he didn't need or want it. That brought me down to $24,850. But I had forgotten a $100 amount to the Council for a Livable World; and I hadn't bothered to list $25 to the DNC and $15 to the

RNC (I like to receive their mailings), so my presumed total was $24,990. But herewith the six transgressions:

1. The $500 pledge to Pell mentioned in my 11/4 letter.

2. The $100 gift on my behalf by Harold Willens to Ron Dellums.

3. In 1977 I gave $500 each to Russ Hemenway and Bella Abzug to help them seek the 18th C.D. nomination for the vacant Koch seat. Then when Bella won the nomination, I gave her an additional $500 in January '78. Total of $1500. The young woman who helped me prepare the 10/6/78 list, Karen Kessler, had not realized that the $1500 counted toward my 1978 ceiling of $25,000. The people who supplied her with my records, John Hodgkin and Gertrude Myers, had not flagged the amounts. Russ Hemenway, who sat with me on 10/6 to plan the final donations, didn't remember it. I didn't remember it. On a scale of 1–10, in terms of familiarity with the law and awareness of its provisions, I reckon you'd rate Russ and me at 9, John at 7, Gertrude at 5, Karen (who's new on my staff) at 2. We're all guilty as hell. Karen didn't know the difference, being new, but Russ and I know the law well enough to realize that the by-election totals count toward the calendar year totals; so we both violated the law! Incidentally, had the by-election taken place in December 1977, there would have been no violation, right? That sure is a funny, funny law you administer, Neil.

4. Last Friday I did a financial review of my Balance Sheet for 9/30/78 and discovered a startling item: Accounts Receivable, Women's Campaign Fund: $2200. I asked my CPA $ tax advisor staffer, John Hodgkin, to explain it to me. Well, it seems that my bookkeeper Gertrude Myers, who has been a very active volunteer on behalf of the Women's Campaign

Fund, helped run a benefit party here in NYC to raise $$$ for WCF. And, as is normal for groups that I support, money was advanced from my bank account to WCF as "front money" to pay for stamps, printing bills, a paid staffer, and other miscellany to get the benefit party under way. Subsequently, as donations flowed in for the benefit, the advanced $2200 was repaid to my bank. All this took place with only a peripheral awareness on my part. Why? Because it's the *normal* way I help groups I support. I'm in the "business" of philanthropy and public service and its a very ordinary thing for me to advance money in that way. But OOPS, when I do it for a political committee, all of a sudden it's illegal. I forgot. Gertrude and John Hodgkin forgot. We didn't remember that the haunting presence of John Gardner, Common Cause, the FEC, and Supreme Court (& Congress) were all right behind our tracks and would find the whole lot of us ILLEGAL. Damn! I frankly didn't know about it until four days ago. I hasten to report myself and turn myself in. Got the handcuffs ready?

5. A minor item. I gave two fund-raisers for Jim Scheuer in appreciation for all he has done to advance the cause of population in Congress. One was at my D.C. home & office at 122 Maryland, a place where I spend 5–6 days every month. The other was at my family apartment at the Hampshire House in NYC, which is a convenience apartment for family members visiting the Big Apple and for business and personal friends of mine who pass through town. Both are private residence facilities. On each event I spent less than the $500 ceiling on "invitations, food and beverages." But I used two different residences. Seems to me that the spirit of that provision of the FECA was meant to be limited to one residence. True? Any regulations on that? Could I also have had a party here at my current real residence at 800 Park in NYC? And another at the place I'm fixing up to become my

residence for the next several decades at 1133 Fifth in NYC? Can a person have as many as two or even four different "residences" for that provision of the law?

I realize that, not being a candidate or a committee, I'm not entitled under the law to ask for an Advisory Opinion on this point of law, so you guys at the FEC leave characters like me entirely at the mercy of our own very fallible judgements on matters of profound importance like this. So what am I to do? Should I have asked Scheuer to have engaged counsel 5–6 months ago to research this fine point of law and, if no regulation exists, to have sought an Advisory Opinion back in April?

Neil, where's the spontaneity in political participation if Scheuer and Mott should have been *chilled* by the FECA in a decision to have a party which took place only 4 weeks before the actual event?

6. Final minor item. My staff works on these things. My D.C. staff, Anne Zill and Diane Abelman, put in time on political activities. My NYC staff, Karen, Gertrude, John, plus John Cushing, secretary, and Barry Turner, sometimes bartender, all put in staff time on preparing lists of prospective donees, keeping records and accounts on my political participation, planning parties, advising me on who I might donate to. Let's face it. A lot of donors would never bother to report such paid staff time because A) their total annual donations do not brush up against the ceiling of $25,000 per year, or B) because they ambiguously (and fraudulently?) claim that such staff time is "volunteered."

Neil, I must admit to you that if we had kept records on every single time my secretary answered a phone call or letter from a candidate that resulted in a political gift, or every expense for a fund-raising party that fell outside the definition of "invitations, food and beverages" then I'd have to report some $3–5,000 of in-kind giving not allowed by the law. . . .

OK, I've come clean and bared my heart and soul and criminality. What are you going to do about it? I've acknowledged to you that my political participation this year may amount to some $8000 in excess of the legal limits—none of which I was consciously aware of at the time I was doing it. Six different counts of wrong-doing.

Tell me, do you personally think there was anything wrong with my instincts and desires to help the cause of good politics in this country? Do you think I was exercising undue influence over the political process? Was I contributing to the "sense of futility" of the small contributor? Was I engaged in any venal act of self-service? Do I deserve to be chastised, subjected to a criminal proceeding (along with my "accomplices")? Should I go to jail and/or be fined severely?

I can't help but think there are hundreds of can-didates and donors and other participants in the political process in this country who are constantly *chilled* by the provisions of the FECA and are worried continuously by possible infringements of the law. You doubtless get dozens of "mea culpa" letters like this confessing transgressions. How do you handle such admissions of guilt? I'm very curious to know.

Gimme another week or two and I'll probably think of another half-dozen violations.

I stand ready for your indictment!

Stewart

In 1975, when Democratic and Republican candidates were seeking to raise money so as to qualify for matching funds, the FEC announced that they were going to audit my committee's books. We had scarcely begun our campaign and had filed all of the legally required reports. We were not asking for matching funds or federal funds in any form, since we thought we were not eligible for them. There seemed no justification for the audit, which would have distracted our limited staff from its work. Our chairman refused access to our records on the grounds that the audit was unnecessary, irrelevant, and without any legal justification, and my committee asked for an explanation. The commission responded by repeating its demand for access to the records.

A time was set for FEC auditors to come and audit the records to which they would be refused access. The press was asked to come and observe. About an hour before the meeting, the commission called to say they were not coming. Later, when our lawyer met with several of theirs, the commission dropped its demand for a special audit.

Although a television network sent a correspondent and a crew to cover the confrontation, when the FEC failed to show, the crew was withdrawn without reporting the backdown. The explanation given us by the network spokesperson was "no confrontation, no story," even though within weeks, television networks devoted program segments to an empty baseball field in which a World Series game would have been played had rain not postponed it, and a football stadium empty because of a strike by players.

The most serious obstacle to our campaign was the commission's refusal to tell us whether we would be eligible for federal money if we obtained over 5 percent of the vote in the general election, and if so, for what purposes we might use that money. When we made our request, the polls showed that we might get 6 percent or more of the vote.

Although the commission had been quick to give rulings and interpretations when the League of Women Voters was seeking to collect and spend large sums of money in financing the presidential debates, the commission waited nearly six weeks before considering our request—weeks critical to our campaign. And then they deadlocked three to three on a motion to give us the advisory opinion we had requested. Since a tie vote defeats a motion, the three Democrats, voting as a unit against the three Republicans, prevented any action. Without any confirming opinion from the commission, it was impossible to seek credit in anticipation of becoming eligible for pro-rata funds after the elections. Obviously the Democrats sought to hamper our campaign because they feared if we were better financed, we could hurt Carter's candidacy more than Ford's. We did not have time to go to court to force the commission to take up our request.

Meanwhile, the Democratic members of the commission had served the Democratic party well. They had demonstrated their willingness to do so by obstructing a campaign that had the potential of hurting the election chances of their candidate.

When the FEC moves against a candidate or committee, there is heavy pressure on the latter to settle out of court. Quick settlement, surrender in many cases, gets the issue out of the press and gives the impression that the candidate or the committee is trying to abide by the law.

In its defense, the commission cites figures showing that most of its compliance cases are settled without serious protest from those against whom they are filed, without court tests. These reports tell little about whether the demands were reasonable or legal. The FEC allows itself wide discretion in determining procedures and settlements.

For example, mingling campaign funds with personal finances can be a violation of federal law. Such a charge was made against the 1976 Carter campaign committee. In response, the committee paid a fine of $1,950. As in an earlier case, the FEC announced that it had decided that the fine was sufficient because of mitigating circumstances.

The commission also stated that by paying the fine, the Carter committee did not admit that it had "knowingly and willfully" violated any federal laws. Whether or not the Federal Election Commission's original charge was valid was not settled.

Did the FEC make law, or did it fail to enforce the law? Both questions remain unanswered in the settlement of this case.

Persons and organizations charged by the commission face a difficult choice. They can surrender, wholly or in part, to the commission by agreeing with the commission's findings that a violation of the law has occurred (either admitting guilt, or as in the case of the Carter committee, without admitting guilt) and paying a fine, or they can resist. The latter involves court proceedings that can be very expensive and are almost certain to draw adverse press and media coverage. As a rule, the charge of a violation receives more attention than its resolution or dismissal.

Even the national committees of the two major parties have had trouble handling the many legal problems raised by the statute, as have strong organizations like the American Civil Liberties Union, corporations, and corporate political action committees. Private citizens, third-party candidates and their committees, and independents with inadequate financing find it difficult to bear the expense of conducting a case against the government-financed Federal Election Commission and its lawyers. Consequently, they are inclined to surrender, a procedure that is bad in itself and dangerous in the long run. What may seem to be a minor concession in a single campaign when added to other small concessions can have a most serious effect on the political process.

Such concessions encourage the commission to assume more and more lawmaking powers as precedents of surrender build and are referred to in subsequent, comparable cases. The process is a low-level demonstration of what Pastor Martin Niemoller, who was a member of the Nazi opposition movement in Germany, described as the dangerous practice of taking the easy way out as long as one's own interests are not seriously affected. Niemoller cited his own passivity as the Nazis moved against other persons and groups in German society, until finally they turned on Lutheran ministers.

The Federal Election Commission, even when enforcing the federal election law literally and without discretion, can seriously affect the outcome of an election. Timing and the manner in which charges are presented can be crucial. A good example was the application of federal election law to the presidential campaign of the governor of Pennsylvania, Milton Shapp, in 1976. In order for Governor Shapp to qualify for matching funds and for the recognition that went with raising $5,000 in each of twenty states, a Shapp campaign fund-raiser allegedly promised to reimburse a Georgia donor for a contribution needed to fill the Georgia quota. It was also alleged that a fund-raiser asked an Alabama textile plant manager to supply letters from employees saying that they had made $100 contributions to the Shapp campaign when they had not done so. There were similar allegations about Shapp fund-raising in other states.

The Federal Election Commission charged that the Shapp forces were responsible for irregular contributions in five of the twenty states. There could have been two pressures for the illegal actions: financial, which in the case of Shapp must be discounted because of his willingness to spend his own money; and recognition, since qualification in twenty states was followed by a grant of matching funds and assignment of Secret Service protection. Shapp was eventually ordered to return approximately $300,000 of matching funds to the federal government, which he did, using a personal check. Shapp himself was not charged with violating the law. But many persons involved in the irregular fund-raising were fined by the FEC, and a few were prosecuted by the Justice Department. Shapp, a millionaire, dropped out of the presidential race in March 1976, saying that he could not raise sufficient funds for his campaign under the restrictions of the federal election law; Julian Bond gave the same reason for not entering the campaign.

In October 1977, the Republicans, who had gone along with the passage of the campaign act and the granting of powers to the FEC in the belief that they had a firm and continuing understanding with the Democrats that Republicans would name Republican members of the FEC, were brought to realize that a two-party system preserved by laws reflecting political arrangements can be changed by law and by political action.

The Republicans were shocked by political realities. The issue arose over a prospective appointment to fill a Republican vacancy on the commission. According to newspaper reports, Republican Senate leader Howard Baker and Republican House leader John Rhodes met with President Carter and came away believing that Carter understood the arrangement honored by President Ford, namely, that recommendations of party leaders would be accepted. The Republicans submitted the names of the two possible appointees to fill the Republican vacancy on the commission. Carter reportedly was unhappy with the suggested appointees because both were opposed to public funding of congressional campaigns. Carter subsequently wrote Baker and Rhodes requesting ten or twelve additional names for his consideration, adding that he expected those named to "be generally sympathetic" to the aims of the FEC, including financial disclosure and public financing.

Later the Republicans submitted a third name, that of
former Representative Charlotte Reid, but did not supply
the number suggested by Carter. Without consultation with
the Republicans, Carter announced his nomination of Sam
Zagoria for the Republican vacancy on the commission.
There was Republican objection to Zagoria on two
grounds. The first objection was that he was not a bona fide
Republican (he had been an aide to liberal Republican
Senator Clifford Case of New Jersey, he had been head of
the Newspaper Guild at the *Washington Post* thirty years
earlier, and he had been named as a Republican member
of the National Labor Relations Board by President Johnson). The second objection to the Zagoria nomination was
procedural, in that the Ford precedent had not been followed and the Republican leadership had been ignored.
The practice of appointing nominal Republicans to fill Republican commission posts in Democratic administrations
is well established, as is the reverse in Republican administrations. Carter may have assumed that appointments
to the Federal Election Commission could be made in this
established manner. If this was his thought, he was at
fault on two counts: first, he did not understand that the
Federal Election Commission is qualitatively different
from other commissions in that it controls the political
process itself, and second, that whereas the Republicans
were quite willing to have a commission on which independents (roughly one-third of the population) were un-
represented, they would not yield their claim to their own
party-determined representation. Under pressure, President Carter yielded, leaving the commission as highly politicized as it had been under Ford, but politicized and
balanced within the limits of two-party politics.

Tight partisan control over the commission was demonstrated also in the handling of Commissioner Neil Staebler,
a Democrat whose term was expiring about the time that

the Zagoria nomination came up. Staebler wanted to be reappointed, but as a commissioner he had cast one vote that displeased those responsible for his appointment. In 1975 he had voted to permit corporations to solicit political contributions from their employees in the same way that the law allowed unions to solicit from their members. This vote displeased organized labor, Democratic party leaders, and, apparently, the President. The President chose not to reappoint Staebler and instead nominated a Mr. John McGarry, a friend of House Speaker Thomas P. O'Neill, Jr. McGarry, it was believed, would make no such mistake of independent judgment as that which brought displeasure on the head of Commissioner Staebler.

As 1980 began, the Congress, which created the FEC, and the press, which accepted it, were beginning to ask questions about the commission. Among the questions were these:

1. Why, although the commission regulates campaign spending of over $500 million per presidential election year, did it have at last count only two certified public accountants on its auditing staff?

2. Why did one of its leading auditors quit, observing on leaving, "I just believe that those people don't know what the hell they're doing"?

3. Why did twenty out of twenty-seven dates set by the staff for preparations for the 1980 campaign pass without any action being taken, even though more than $3 million had already been raised for the 1980 presidential campaign?

4. Why could the commission not account for thousands of dollars in 1976 Carter campaign expenditures that were reported to be incorrectly documented?

5. Why was the audit of the Carter general election campaign so long delayed?

6. Why is the staff turnover of approximately 25 per-

cent annually so much larger than that of most government agencies?

The 1979 chairwoman of the commission, Joan Aikens, conceded that there was a morale problem. She did not explain why it existed or what she intended to do about it. There were charges of cronyism and of political influence in hiring of personnel. Commissioners often intervened in the formulation of advisory opinions by staff lawyers, according to the commission's general counsel, and said "how they want them to come out."

This is roughly the state of the government commission which, with ill-defined powers exercised under great political pressure by incompetent personnel, stands astride the American political process. There is little reason to expect that the Congress will make any significant changes in the federal election laws as they bear on presidential elections. The same pressures that brought about the passage of the laws still obtain, and Congress, not wanting to be held in favor of corruption in politics or considered as having made serious mistakes in the passage of the' election laws, is not yet ready to change them in any significant way.

Change, if it is to be achieved, will have to be accomplished through court actions.

The possibilities of success in the courts are much greater than those of success in Congress.

The experiences in the 1976 campaign established a basis for further court testing of the constitutionality of the federal election laws. This testing was anticipated to some degree by the Supreme Court in its 1976 action when it left the way open to future challenges based on experience with the law. Some of the later challenges were not anticipated by the Court in its 1975–76 examination, because they are based on provisions of the law added by Congress in response to the Court's suggestions and rulings. Other challenges are based on actions by the Federal Election Commission that no one could have anticipated.

The Supreme Court, after voiding limits on expenditures by candidates and campaign committees early in its opinion, later, and without adequate explanation, upheld such limits when accompanied by the acceptance of federal subsidies by candidates. The Court made no effort in its opinion to reconcile that decision with what is called the "unconstitutional-condition doctrine." As Brice Clagett and John Bolton stated in an article in the *Vanderbilt Law Review* of November 1976: "The spectacle of government's demanding that a candidate restrict, in return for federal payments, what the Court itself has squarely held to be his First Amendment right to speech would seem to present one of the strongest cases imaginable for application of the unconstitutional-condition doctrine. Further, the case is strengthened by at least two considerations that as a practical matter will coerce the candidate into accepting subsidies whenever offered and thus into accepting 'voluntary' limits on his speech. First, his subsidy-accepting opponent is relieved of some, or in general elections, all the burdens and uncertainties involved in political fund-raising. Secondly, contribution limits intensify the competitive disadvantages by making private fund-raising far more onerous than ever before."

The core of the abuse of this constitutional right is that the law limits the funds formerly available to a candidate through private fund-raising activity. The government then offers public funds in their stead, thus making what had been a private activity a "state action" subject to government control. Limitations on freedom of speech are, in effect, purchased and paid for by the government itself. Clagett and Bolton observed, "When this process involves a virtually coerced surrender of first amendment rights in an area going to the heart of the political process, it is difficult to see how the Court's unexplained result can be sustained if the issue is brought before it and fully analyzed."

The fact that the Court rested its case for the limitation of contributions to $1,000 per person per candidate and to $5,000 per committee per candidate, on the grounds that these limitations would eliminate corruption and the appearance of corruption, leaves the way open to further challenges on the grounds that experience with the law does not sustain the contention of those who supported it. Moreover, the contribution limitations are open to the challenge that they favor wealthy candidates and that the uncertain line drawn between independent expenditures by individuals and expenditures under the control of candidates or their committees leads to additional discrimination and inequity.

A second area of challenge to which the Court might be responsive is that of disclosure. In 1975 it was argued before the Supreme Court that the disclosure of the names of contributors might discourage them and lead to harassment. The Court acknowledged both possibilities and indicated that, in examining the record under the act, courts need not be overly strict in their requirements of proofs of harassment by parties with unpopular ideologies.

More difficult to prove, but inherently more dangerous in its potential to discourage significant and potentially successful political efforts, is the chilling effect of disclosure of contributions to parties or candidacies which are closer in purpose and in program to the purposes and programs of the two major parties, especially when such third parties might draw off enough votes to cause defeat, or appear to cause defeat, to a major party. It is more respectable and politically safer to be on the record as a contributor to what is labeled an "ideological party," Socialist, Vegetarian, Prohibitionist, and the like, than to be recorded as a contributor to a political movement that might cause the defeat of either Republican or Democratic candidates.

The most significant and important prospective challenge to the federal election laws, however, is to the actual operations of the Federal Election Commission, because that challenge reaches to the heart of the constitutional principle of separation of powers. When the Supreme Court was asked to rule on this point in 1975, it sidestepped the issue by finding that the FEC was improperly appointed.

The Federal Election Commission, following the Supreme Court decision in early 1976, was reconstituted in a constitutional way. The test now is of the constitutionality of its operation. First, can the Congress retain and exercise a "legislative veto" over the actions of an independent agency? Second, has the commission been given, or exercised, extraconstitutional or unconstitutional authority in its interpretations and enforcement of the federal election laws?

In making their argument before the Supreme Court in 1975, in the case of *Buckley* v. *Valeo,* our lawyers attacked a provision of the law which allowed rulings and interpretations of the Federal Election Commission to stand unless they were overruled or "vetoed" by either the House of Representatives or the Senate. They said the provision was an unconstitutional violation of the principle of separation of powers, and, because the veto could be used by incumbent House and Senate members while their reelection campaigns were in progress, that it also gave excessive power to incumbents over their challengers. The Court declined to rule on either point; it simply held that, as constituted, the commission could not exercise rule-making powers.

The "legislative veto" has been included in many laws, since the passage of the Reorganization Act of 1939, but not until *Buckley* v. *Valeo* had it been challenged in court. The constitutional argument against permitting the legislative veto is that to allow a rule considered to be legislative in nature to stand (the House or Senate having failed or refused to veto it) is to establish a law without constitutionally required presidential participation in the legislative act. If the rule is judged to be executive, then the exercise of the legislative veto over it is an unconstitutional intrusion of the legislative branch into the area of executive responsibility.

Clagett and Bolton, in their article on *Buckley* v. *Valeo* in the *Vanderbilt Law Review* of November 1976, summarized the case against the constitutionality of the legislative veto with these points: first, "in this instance the congressional veto operates within the ambit of the First Amendment, an area in which the presumption of constitutionality is much weaker than in other areas," and second, "the legislators' intense personal interest in the substance of Commission regulations should cause courts to pause and consider the possible harm such a veto might inflict on our relatively open political system."

Clagett and Bolton cite experts who argue that when a President has approved legislation allowing the Congress veto power, or when such legislation has been passed over his own veto, that power has properly been given to Congress. According to this theory, the power belongs to the office, not to the man, and once passed can be used by the person or body to which it has been given. One can only conclude from a careful reading and rereading of this interpretation of the Constitution that a President is permitted to perform unconstitutional acts that are binding on him and on subsequent Presidents.

Such an interpretation is far from that which was given to the separation-of-powers principle by the men who drafted the Constitution and who gave special attention to protecting and defining the President's veto power in Article I, Section 7, of the Constitution. It provides that "every order, resolution, or vote to which the concurrence of the Senate and House of Representatives may be necessary (except on a question of adjournment) shall be presented to the President of the United States; and before the same shall take effect, shall be approved by him, or being disapproved by him, shall be repassed by two-thirds of the Senate and House of Representatives, according to the rules and limitations prescribed in the case of a bill."

James Madison, speaking in the constitutional convention, indicated that the provision was carefully worded to prevent the possibility that a presidential veto could be made meaningless, since, he said, if the presidential veto were confined to bills, "it would be evaded by acts under the form and name of resolutions, votes, etc. . . ."

Hamilton, too, in the *Federalist* No. 73, sustained the same position. After writing of the propensity and danger of legislative encroachment on the executive branch, he added, "From these clear and indubitable principles results the propriety of a negative, either absolute or qualified, in the Executive, upon the acts of the legislative branches."

President Ford, who signed the bill giving Congress a legislative veto over FEC regulations, and President Carter, who has accepted it in operation, have prejudiced their own powers under the Constitution. They have left to the courts the settlement on constitutional grounds of an issue which should never have been presented for such decision.

States' Rights and Wrongs

Legislatures in many states have moved, especially in this century, to give advantages and preferences to the Republican and Democratic parties and to limit freedom of political action of third parties and independent candidates.

Republican and Democratic partisans have shared the action. Some of the restrictive laws were prompted by unhappy Republicans, such as those passed in some states following the Bull Moose efforts of Teddy Roosevelt. Some were prompted by the anti-party movements of the twenties, such as the Progressives, who were a threat to both parties. The limited successes of Henry Wallace and George Wallace in presidential campaigns also moved some state legislatures to defensive and protective response, until by 1976 at least half of the states of the Union had laws giving advantages to the Republican and Democratic parties. They ranged from marginal advantages to those that practically eliminated the possibility of effective challenge.

The usual argument for restrictive legislation, an argument that is not borne out by history or by theory, is that two-party politics makes for good government.

In 1780, John Adams, writing to a friend about the newly adopted Massachusetts constitution (a document that Adams helped to draft), observed, "There is nothing which I dread so much as a division of the Republic into two great parties, each arranged under its leader, and concerting measures in opposition to each other. This, in my humble apprehension, is to be dreaded as the greatest political evil under our Constitution."

The country and its political thinkers have come a long way from Adams and his warnings about partisanship.

In 1974, an election official for the state of Kansas wrote, "At this time nominations for presidential electors may be made only by a delegate or mass convention of a political party having a national or state organization."

The Michigan director of elections said: "In Michigan, there is no way a name of a candidate can appear on the ballot for the office of President and Vice-President, without a political party of some nature being formed prior thereto."

A Nebraska official stated: "Because we have two recognized parties in Nebraska, the electoral college is appointed by the parties."

The assistant attorney general of Utah, citing a court decision, said: "The nomination of presidential electors may be made solely by political party conventions."

The assistant supervisor of elections in the state of Washington said: "The state of Washington, at this time, does not provide access to a primary or general election ballot for an 'independent' candidate."

Not all of the restrictive state laws absolutely prevent independent candidates or candidates of third parties from having access to the ballot. But they do impose conditions that are all but impossible to meet, such as early filing dates, unreasonable numbers of petition signatures, limited times during which signatures may be gathered, unreasonable requirements for the validation of signatures, and requirements that signatures be gathered from scattered jurisdictions and counties, congressional districts, towns, and even magistrate districts, and so forth.

Over the years state laws have been challenged in the courts. Some legal victories have been won but usually have been short-lived, as legislatures have moved to pass new legislation, often also subject to legal challenge.

In 1968, restrictions on third-party rights were challenged principally by the American Independent party, the George Wallace organization. That party was able to gain ballot access in fifty states only after strenuous and expensive petition campaigns and several lawsuits. The most important test in that year was the case brought by the Wallace party and the Socialist Labor party against a whole complex of Ohio election laws that effectively denied ballot access to third parties, independents, and write-in candidates.

Williams v. *Rhodes* (as the case was known) should have become a landmark, bringing about the rejection of state-controlled two-party politics. In its decision the U.S. Supreme Court noted that Ohio "claims that the State may validly promote a two-party system in order to encourage compromise and political stability. The fact is, however, that the Ohio system does not merely favor a 'two-party system'; it favors two particular parties—the Republicans and the Democrats—and in effect tends to give them a complete monopoly. There is, of course, no reason why two parties should retain a permanent monopoly on the right to have people vote for or against them. Competition in ideas and governmental policies is at the core of our electoral process and of the First Amendment freedoms. . . ."

The Court held that "the totality of the Ohio restrictive laws taken as a whole imposes a burden on voting and the associational rights which we hold is an invidious discrimination, in violation of the Equal Protection Clause."

The thrust of the *Williams* v. *Rhodes* decision was not maintained in later Supreme Court rulings dealing with restrictive state laws. Thus, in *Maryland People's Party* v. *Mandel* in 1973, the Court upheld a Maryland law that required third parties to file their petitions by March of a presidential election year and to organize in every county of the state.

In 1974, in the case of *American Party of Texas* v. *White,* the Court upheld a law that required minor parties to choose their candidates by convention rather than by primary (unlike the major parties) and that subsidized the primaries of major parties but not the conventions of minor parties. Moreover, persons who had voted in a party's primary were barred from signing for independent candidates.

The People's party, which ran Dr. Benjamin Spock for the presidency in 1972, had difficulties similar to those of George Wallace in 1968. In an article published in *Progressive* magazine in 1975, David Anderson and Jim McClellan, campaign managers for the Spock campaign, wrote, "Spock—and the people who struggled with fifty-one different election laws in fifty states and the District of Columbia to get his name on the ballot—learned one thing from the 1972 campaign: Despite their declining influence with the electorate, the two parties still control access to the ballot. Hostile state election officials, discriminatory election laws, and an institutionalized two-party system all worked together to hinder access to the ballot."

After describing the specific problems faced in Arizona, Indiana, New Hampshire, Pennsylvania, and Utah, Andersen and McClellan added this commentary: "Though there is often recourse to the courts and an eventual judicial victory, the process—like the conspiracy trials visited on the anti-war movement by the government—is time-consuming and financially draining, deflecting much energy from the campaign. Also, in the case of elections, there is a time factor. While it may have been reassuring when a court ruled in the spring of 1974 that Spock was wrongfully excluded from the 1972 ballot in Hawaii, or when an appeals court determined in August 1974 that the District of Columbia had erred in refusing to count votes cast for the Spock-Hobson ticket, the damage was done and irreversible."

At the beginning of my own independent campaign for the presidency in 1976, we knew we would have some trouble in getting ballot placement, but we expected to be on the ballot in at least forty states. We finally made it in only twenty-nine. In one or two cases, failure was properly attributable to our technical and legal mistakes. In most of them, however, failure was due to our lack of money for organizing petition drives (thanks to restrictions of the federal election laws); to the manner in which state laws were interpreted and enforced against us; and to the unexpectedly strong efforts on the part of the Democratic party to prevent our getting on the ballot, efforts which in at least one case involved shocking and disturbing support from the state courts. Because of these obstacles, most of our time and energy in the campaign of 1976 was spent on court proceedings and in efforts to obtain ballot placement, rather than in actual campaigning.

As a result of legal maneuvers in 1976, parts of the election laws of eighteen states were altered or struck down on constitutional grounds. The list that follows shows what the legal obstacles were and what the courts did about them.

> **Delaware**—Federal court, in *McCarthy* v. *Tribbitt,* found unconstitutional the state's prohibition of independent candidacy. Delaware has since established a procedure whereby independents may qualify for the ballot.

> **Florida**—Federal court, in *McCarthy* v. *Askew,* struck down prohibition of independent candidacy. Florida now has an independent route to the ballot.

> **Idaho**—Although federal court denied relief before

election, state conceded, in *McCarthy* v. *Andrus,* that its prohibition of independent candidacy was unconstitutional. Idaho now has a system for qualifying independent candidates.

Illinois—State reinterpreted its law, after *McCarthy* v. *Lunding* suit was filed, to allow independent candidacy; suit dismissed by consent.

Iowa—State reversed, under threat of McCarthy legal challenge, an opinion of its solicitor general that would have raised petition signature requirement from 1,000 to approximately 20,000. And in *McCarthy* v. *Kopel,* federal court found unconstitutional a state law that provided free voter lists to Democrats and Republicans, but not to independents.

Kansas—State entered into consent decree in federal court, in *McCarthy* v. *Shanahan,* to terminate its prohibition of independent candidacy.

Louisiana—In *McCarthy* v. *Hardy,* federal court moved back deadline for petitions, due to election officials' failure to provide accurate information on deadline.

Massachusetts—In *McCarthy* v. *Secretary of the Commonwealth,* state court found that McCarthy forces had filed enough signatures; also established right of appeal when local election boards strike valid signatures. Judgment affirmed by highest state court.

Michigan—Three-judge federal court, in *McCarthy* v. *Austin,* found unconstitutional the prohibition of independent candidacy.

Missouri—Federal court struck down prohibition of independent candidacy and deadline, and ruled McCarthy petition signatures sufficient, in *McCarthy* v. *Kirkpatrick.* A new Missouri law affirms the court victory.

Nebraska—In *McCarthy* v. *Exon,* three-judge federal court struck down prohibition of independent candidacy; judgment affirmed by U.S. Supreme Court. Nebraska now has a process for independents.

New Mexico—In post-election decision on *McCarthy* v. *Evans,* federal court found unconstitutional the state's ban on independent candidacy. New Mexico has since established a process for independents.

Oklahoma—State supreme court, in *McCarthy* v. *Slater,* struck down state law barring independent candidacy. Oklahoma now has a qualifying procedure for independents.

Rhode Island—Federal court, in *McCarthy* v. *Noel,* struck down August 12 deadline.

Tennessee—State court ruled, in *McCarthy* v. *Hassler,* that state must place independent candidate's name on ballot with his elector candidates.

Texas—In *McCarthy* v. *Briscoe,* three-judge federal court found unconstitutional the prohibition of independent candidacy, but denied relief; court of appeals denied relief; U.S. Supreme Court granted relief. Texas now has an independent route to the ballot.

Utah—Federal court, in *McCarthy* v. *Rampton,* struck down prohibition of independent candidacy.

Vermont—Federal court ordered state, in *McCarthy* v. *Salmon,* to accept petitions certified by town clerks after deadline.

Many of these cases would not have been necessary if state laws had been brought in line with court rulings such as *Storer* v. *Brown* in 1974. In that case the Supreme Court rejected the argument that a state may require an independent candidate either to join a political party or to form a new one in order to run for the presidency. The Court wrote:

"But more fundamentally, the candidate, who is by definition an independent and desires to remain one, must now
consider himself a party man, surrendering his independent
status. Must he necessarily choose the political party route
if he wants to appear on the ballot in the general election?
We think not." Despite this clear ruling and the clear language, at the beginning of 1976 thirteen states barred independent candidacies for the presidency.

Two states conceded the unconstitutionality of their statute in court after suits were filed in 1976, and one conceded
the unconstitutionality of its law, but only after the election
was over. In one state, we were unable to find the legal
assistance needed to challenge the law. Nine states refused
to concede, forcing litigation, which in three cases reached
the Supreme Court. One of these cases—the *McCarthy* v.
Briscoe case in Texas—was taken to the Supreme Court
following a circuit court decision that the law was clearly
unconstitutional, but the court would allow the state to
ignore the Constitution because of the time factor. A Texas
election official commented that his agency was not capable
of rearranging the balloting procedure (we called it "a declaration of his own incompetence"), which scarcely seemed
valid grounds for ignoring the Constitution of the United
States.

Justice Powell, in an in-chambers opinion (with which
four other justices indicated agreement), expressed approval of the decision of the lower court. He wrote, "In
view of these pronouncements, the District Court was fully
justified in characterizing the new Texas law—enacted
little more than a year after *Storer* and *Lubin* were decided
—as demonstrating an 'intransigent and discriminatory position' and an 'incomprehensible policy.' " The Supreme
Court ordered that my name be placed on the ballot.

In a Michigan case in 1976, the state ignored the 1974
Storer v. *Brown* ruling and argued from earlier decisions.

Then two members of a three-judge federal court in Michigan agreed to the obvious, that the *Storer* decision was binding. The state conceded that our petition signatures would have been accepted and counted had our supporters been willing to call themselves a party. The court, in rejecting that condition, declared, "An integral part of an independent candidate's message is his freedom from partisan ties. Even the nominal admission of partisan affiliation required by the Michigan election laws seriously compromises an independent candidate's credibility. More importantly, it penalizes him for acting in concert with his ideology by denying him an opportunity extended to similarly situated candidates not opposed to partisan affiliation. In addition to denying independent candidates and their electors the opportunity to appear on the ballot, such a scheme impairs the ability of voters to effectively register their opposition to partisan policies or practices. The restriction of the rights of independents to equal political expression and association serves no legitimate governmental interest and cannot be sustained."

These cases are important not only in campaigns for the presidency or the vice-presidency. They have a bearing on the rights of persons who might have run for any of approximately 125,000 elective offices at the federal, state, or local level. Attorney John C. Armor of Baltimore, who coordinated our 1976 legal challenges, estimated that from 20,000 to 45,000 of these offices were still barred to independent candidates by state law in 1977.

Of all fifty states in 1976, Delaware had the most restrictive law regarding independents. It prevented them from running for any office except delegate to state constitutional conventions. While this limitation, as it applied to presidential candidates in Delaware, was removed in 1976, it remained in effect for other offices. According to John

Armor's 1977 report, no one could run for coroner or for dog-catcher in Dover, Delaware, as an independent.

Flat prohibition of independent candidacies was the most common basis for action in the 1976 court cases. There were other provisions of state election laws that were successfully challenged, and some that went unchallenged for want of time, money, and volunteer legal counsel.

Early filing deadlines are one device used by states to inhibit and hamper independent and third-party political action. Pennsylvania, for example, before 1976, required filings in February of the election year, long before political realities had shaped up and long before the established parties had to make similar decisions about their candidates. In the case of *Salera* v. *Tucker*, in 1976, the Supreme Court upheld a lower court decision which had struck down the February deadline requirement but did not lay down guidelines as to what would be a reasonable or constitutionally acceptable filing date.

It appears as though final resolution will have to come from the Supreme Court because of the intransigence of the state legislatures, which seem unable or unwilling to respond to the obvious directions implicit in such court decisions as *Bradley* v. *Mandel*, involving a U.S. Senate candidate in Maryland in 1976. In this case the district court pointed out the obvious fact that "signature gathering by an independent candidate . . . is the equivalent of the primary election. Maryland's equal treatment would have validity only if the deadline for the filing of petitions was the same date as the primary election, but it is not."

Laws providing unreasonable deadlines for filing petitions were also challenged successfully by a local candidate in Arkansas and by our campaigns in Rhode Island and Missouri. We won other issues in Louisiana, Massachusetts, Tennessee, and Vermont. A decision in the Missouri case was most comprehensive and thorough. It struck the prohibition against independents and the unreasonably early filing date, and it dealt as well with the practical matters of counting and verifying signatures.

In 1976 third-party organizations experienced difficulties similar to those encountered by independents. In California, the requirement for a new party to qualify was about 600,000 valid signatures. Because of potential errors in signings, it is necessary to get, as a rule, three signatures in order to be sure that two will pass the test of examination. In California, to meet this level of insurance, it would be necessary to get approximately 900,000 signatures.

The anti-government Libertarian party—young, well organized, and relatively well financed—did not even try. Its presidential candidate, Roger MacBride, did qualify by submitting more than the 100,000 signatures required of an independent candidate. Obviously, the requirements are unreasonable, both as to the number of signatures and as to the time prescribed for soliciting them. The law was to be faulted not only on these two points but on a further requirement, that petitions had to be circulated by city or town. The law now requires that the petitions may be circulated by county. This provision, although burdensome, is more reasonable than the town and county provisions of the old law.

In Georgia, the required number of signatures was over 100,000, a number that the Libertarians and others despaired of getting.

In 1976, in Maine, where 11,000 valid signatures were required, the Communist party filed 13,000 signatures. Nonetheless, the Communist party was thrown off the ballot, possibly on the assumption that it had cheated, because no one believed there could actually be that many persons in Maine who favored having the Communist candidates on the ballot.

Not only were the laws confusing and difficult, if not impossible, to comply with, but in a number of states, notably California and Michigan, the laws were in the process of being changed while the campaign was going on. The troubles of those who circulated petitions read like a political version of the Book of Job. In New Hampshire, for example, although the number of signatures required was reasonable, the process by which they had to be verified was extremely difficult to comply with. First, a petition form was not approved by the New Hampshire election officials until May. Second, the petition form did not allow for a group of signers, say ten or twenty; each petition had space for just one voter's signature, and each signature had to be certified by two election supervisors from the voter's town or residence. This meant that either the petition signer or the solicitor had to locate two election supervisors and obtain the certification before the petition could be filed with the secretary of state of New Hampshire. Despite these difficulties, 1,190 signed and certified petitions were gathered in New Hampshire.

Kentucky presented a different problem. Only 1,000 signatures were needed for independent ballot placement, and the date for filing, according to a literal reading of the law, was September 8. However, on March 25, 1976, the attorney general's office told us that they had interpreted the law to mean that the deadline was not September 8, but March 31, less than a week away. Though a court test was a possibility and would probably have been won, we opted for an all-out effort to get the 1,000 signatures and managed to do so in the limited time.

One of the greatest achievements in grass-roots independent political history was the work of volunteers in getting the necessary signatures in Arizona. The Arizona law relative to independents is vague. In early attempts to interpret it, five lawyers gave five different interpretations.

The Arizona committee members decided that they would accept the most rigorous interpretation, under which it was held, first, that approximately 6,500 signatures would be necessary, and second, that most of the petitions would have to be circulated and signed within a ten-day period following the primary election (from September 7 through September 17), and that independents as well as Republicans and Democrats could sign the nominating petition. On the other hand, if a Democrat or a Republican had voted in the primary nominating petition earlier in the year, he could not sign a petition to nominate an independent candidate for President.

Just to find a person eligible to sign required an inquiry involving five or six questions. Despite all of these limitations, 13,000 persons were found willing to sign the petitions.

The Iowa effort was a nightmare of obstructionism, changed rulings from state officials, modified petition forms, and change in the number of required signatures, but it ended in a successful petition drive.

The two states in which opposition was most clearly political were Massachusetts and New York. In Massachusetts the Democratic party's prolonged effort to invalidate signatures and deny access to the ballot failed. In New York, after a similar challenge, the petition signatures were declared valid by the state election board. The representatives of the Democratic party took the board decision to a state court, which overruled the board's decision. On appeal the lower court's decision was reversed, but on a third appeal, the highest New York court, a few days before the November election, struck my name from the ballot.

In 1976 a final test of the integrity of state election laws was made by persons who attempted to write in their presidential choice where write-in voting was permitted. Write-in voting, it turned out, is all but impossible where voting machines are used. One state law required that the names of all presidential electors committed to support a candidate not on the ballot be written into the machine through an opening, allowing access to a piece of paper about the size of a small matchbook. Persons in charge of the voting machines were unable or unwilling to demonstrate how write-in votes might be registered. Excerpts from these two letters from New York are indicative of the experience of a person who tried to write in his vote.

> Tuesday afternoon, when I voted in my local firehouse and I inquired as to the proper procedure for a write-in vote, I was subjected to harassment, scorn and ridicule. Without going into details, I find this completely abhorrent to the ideals of individual liberty and freedom of choice. Had I been a person that was easily intimidated, I would have at best not have been able to vote for my choice, and at worst possibly lost my franchise. Fortunately, I was able to exercise my right, but I feel this type of situation should be made public and this insidious practice must be nipped in the bud. There should also be some standardized procedures and simplified instructions for those who wish to choose this method.

The second letter was as follows:

> On Tuesday November 2, around 7:30 P.M. I went to the Seaman's Institute with the intention of voting. Before signing my name, I asked if it were possible for me to cast a write-in vote. One of the women told me she didn't know how to operate the machine for that. In the course of my inquiries I was told there was no one we could contact to find out the procedure; the paper ballot had certain names on it, and only those could be voted for; besides she couldn't let me use the only one she had. When I asked why I couldn't use

one of the fifty or so I saw in a stack behind her, another of the Deputies asked me to sign the book. While
I was signing I was told they had been instructed to
void any votes for Eugene McCarthy. I asked if I
could simply write who I wanted to vote for on a piece
of paper. No, I had signed the book, I had to vote
on the machine. . . .

I left thinking there was nothing I could do except
to register a complaint which I do now, though the
complaint hardly contains the outrage I feel.

Most of these obstacles to independent and third-party
political action and even abuse of voting rights went un-
reported by the press and unnoted in editorial comment.

The consensus of the twenty-five attorneys who were
involved in legal challenges to state election laws in 1976
is that wherever possible the challenges should be brought
in federal courts.

There are two main reasons for this conclusion. The
first is political: state judges are more immediately and
directly dependent on political parties than are the federal
judges. Their terms of office are generally limited. They
have to be elected and reelected, or, if appointed, appointed by Republican or Democratic officeholders, with
few exceptions. Expecting an anti-party ruling from a
judge so chosen or appointed is expecting a lot. Judges
who would have asked to be excused from a case involving conflict of economic interest did not, on the record
of 1976, even seem to raise a question as to whether
they should sit on a political case in which judgment might
clearly favor their own career and political interests. Judges
on the federal bench, who are selected by virtue of political
identification but whose appointments are for life, can be
expected to be somewhat more free from political considerations in making judgments on cases that might ad-
versely affect the political parties which nurtured them

and brought them to the high bench of the federal courts.

The second reason for going to the federal courts whenever possible is a practical one. Most of the challenges to state law are based on the United States Constitution. While state courts are bound to uphold the Constitution, the overall record shows that the federal courts are more responsive and more reliable in dealing with constitutional issues. This is partly because they generally have had much more experience with constitutional questions and also because of the experience and size of their supporting staffs and the availability of their libraries of federal decisions and constitutional law. Federal court judges, either with or without ambition or hopes for higher positions in the court system, are generally concerned about their reputations as constitutional experts and hopeful that language in their opinions may catch on as principles and precedents for interpretation of the Constitution.

It is obvious from this limited review of the state laws affecting independent and third-party politics that, unless the country is to be bound over to Republican and Democratic party–controlled politics, national rules of procedure are necessary.

The Fourth Estate
Becomes the First Estate

From infallibility to the seal of the confessional

The American "free press" is more fiction than fact. Unbridled and open communication through the press is limited, first because in most major population centers newspapers are monopolies, and second, because major newspapers, as a rule, operate within a corporate form which emphasizes economic gain and profitability as the relevant standards of success. Third, the press does not clearly understand its role in American society.

The press has apparently come to think of itself as an institutionalized Fourth Estate, with special powers and privileges never granted to it by the Constitution or by statute. The powers and privileges once exercised by the church as the First Estate in medieval society now belong to the press.

In a country without an established religion or a recognized infallible head of the church, the press claims a comparable function—to speak arbitrarily, which is to say "ex cathedra," that term here called "the editor's chair."

The press has its own form of dreaded Index according to which it censors news and gives readers only what is good for them to know. "All the news that's fit to print," declares the *New York Times*. One can fairly ask by whose determination? Fit for whom? Fit for what? As medieval inquisitors decided what people should believe, so do newspapers decide who is and is not newsworthy, who is to be made much of or little of or nothing of. The press can give the secular equivalents of "beatification," "canonization," and the "interdict"; it can "excommunicate" and even "condemn," though it still does not dare burn at the stake.

In its insistence on the protection of its sources, the press exercises a version of the "seal of the confessional." (Occasionally a reporter does choose to go to jail rather than reveal sources, as in the recent case of M. A. Farber, a *New York Times* reporter.) It also claims the right to protect its own from scandal, as in the 1978 case of a *New York Times* report on drug use by White House staff members. The report did not include the fact that at least two *Times* reporters had smoked marijuana in the company of White House staff. Perhaps the *Times* thought that such information about members of the press might cause loss of confidence and prejudice newspaper readers against the press. Imagine!

If the press were, in fact, carrying out a function comparable to that attributed to the church, special privileges and exemptions might be granted. But the record of the press over the past twenty years does not lend evidence to support the granting of such special status. The press has failed as an important influence on major social and political issues of the past two decades.

Alfred Friendly, in the *Washington Post* on February 13, 1977, attempted to explain and excuse the press for its building up of the whole anti-Communist cold-war attitude of the early fifties. Friendly acknowledged that within a month after Senator Joseph McCarthy's famous Wheeling, West Virginia, Lincoln Day speech in February 1950, it was clear that he was using fraudulent material (it was actually a rewrite of a Nixon speech given to him by the Republican National Committee). Yet, major newspapers continued to give McCarthy the kind of front-page attention usually reserved for the President of the United States.

Friendly said, "At the outset, for the first week or so, and before they could be examined, McCarthy's charges appeared to be of the most profound national security significance and might, quite possibly, be true." The Senate then panicked and held hearings. "For the press to have ignored the most newsworthy event in the Congress (however phony the thing was beginning to look), the focus of congressional and, almost at once, national attention, is preposterous." Friendly is right. No one expected the press to ignore the story. The point of criticism is its exploitation, its overpublication, of nearly every charge that was made by McCarthy. In contrast is the way the press reported Congressman Hale Boggs's charge some twenty years later that the FBI was spying on members of Congress. When the congressman did not name the people involved and publicly prove his point as requested, the press generally rejected his statement as irresponsible and untrue. Subsequently, he was shown to have been correct. One can only speculate as to what might have happened if the press had only insisted on comparable proof from Senator Joseph McCarthy in 1950.

A disastrously wounding failure on the part of the press was in its coverage of the Vietnam War. Long after there was massive evidence that the administration, especially Dean Rusk and Robert McNamara, did not know what they were talking about in stating needs, in describing events in Vietnam, the press dutifully headlined their every statement. It accepted handouts, reports of success and of progress, almost without challenge or question. All of this was passed on to the public. Most newspapers continued to support the war well into 1969 despite the reports of reliable reporters who were covering the war in Vietnam itself.

Most of the press appeared not to have discovered the truth about the war in Vietnam until after the publication of the Pentagon Papers. Their publication was widely called a heroic act in the name of freedom of the press. The only risk faced by the press was financial, in the possibility that it would have to defend itself against the government in court, but the case was soon settled in the press's favor against a pre-publication federal injunction. In any case, there was little that was surprising in the Papers. To discover that persons in the Pentagon had actually talked against the war should not have been surprising. That there were plans to stifle criticism, and at the same time doubts and disagreements; that the whole truth was not told either to Congress or to the American people—this certainly was not surprising news. Nor was the information, if published, a threat to the national security. The publication of the Papers was billed as a great act of heroic journalism, when in fact what was contained in the reports was familiar, and almost irrelevant.

Haynes Johnson, writing in the *Washington Post* of June 24, 1973, accuses the press of lack of vigor and of general subservience to government policies and programs. The press, Johnson wrote, during the Vietnam War, "was a willing accomplice of government secrecy, official trial balloons, and justifications for policy failures. It was, for the most part, a staunch supporter of government policies, especially in foreign affairs." He also noted the dangers to a reporter in letting himself or herself be taken into the inner ring. "Journalists," he wrote, "came to like the informality and the close association with the cream of Washington officialdom. Out-of-town publishers and editors relished having their men in Washington set up meetings with major figures, including an occasional presidential session."

White House invitations, preserved in permanent plastic,

mounted on the mantels of editors' homes or on the desks of their offices, should be seen as signs of surrender rather than achievement. A few truly professional newspersons refuse to participate in "background meetings." One of these was Doris Fleeson, who held that the backgrounder corrupted.

In radio and television coverage of political campaigns, reporters and correspondents (it is better to be a correspondent, although no one explains what the difference is) are assigned to candidates—as a rule, early in campaigns. A reporter who covers the successful candidate for President usually becomes a White House correspondent after the candidate is installed in office.

In much the same way that the press supported the deeper and deeper involvement in Vietnam and the war, so too it supported, for twenty years, the "cold war" with China. Theodore White, in his book *In Search of History*, writes that his reports on the corruption and incompetence of the Chiang Kai-shek regime were suppressed by Henry Luce, publisher of *Time* magazine. White accepted the suppression of his stories, although he says he threatened to quit. Instead, he shifted to combat reporting, which freed him from the moral burden of political reporting.

The press generally has taken deep bows for the coverage of the Watergate case and the resignation of Richard Nixon. In fact, the pursuit of the case was almost an accident at the start, and afterward it was an act of continuing perseverance by two reporters, Bob Woodward and Carl Bernstein, sustained eventually by their newspaper editor and publisher, rather than an achievement to be credited to the press generally.

According to George Gallup, a month after the break-in at the Democratic Headquarters, only about half of the people in the United States acknowledged having read or heard about Watergate.

Whereas the press is to be credited for following the case, the manner of its pursuit raises serious questions of professionalism and ethics.

It is instructive and interesting to compare the methods used by the "plumbers" of the Nixon campaign with those used by the investigative press, as reported in the Woodward and Bernstein book *All the President's Men*. The "plumbers" used illegal wiretaps; the investigators had people listen to telephone conversations on extension phones. The "plumbers" bugged their subjects; the investigative reporters eavesdropped and used confidential sources. The "plumbers," or the administration, had the FBI check long-distance phone calls with the telephone company; the investigative reporters persuaded sources in the telephone company to give them similar information.

The "plumbers" and their principals were found guilty of obstructing justice; the investigative reporters narrowly escaped prosecution on the charge of tampering with a grand jury.

The "plumbers" broke and entered; the investigative reporters used false identification or misrepresentation of their professional role to get interviews.

The "plumbers" rifled files; the investigative reporters examined, when not watched, what they could find on desks.

The "plumbers," at least some of them, demanded that they be paid off by the Nixon campaign committee; according to their book, the investigative reporters came close to blackmail by threatening to expose informants to superiors.

The "plumbers" sought to justify their actions on the grounds that they were serving a high purpose, the reelection of Richard Nixon. The investigative reporters justified their methods on comparable grounds.

The press, today, sees itself as threatened by lack of respect, by criticism, and particularly by the courts, especially the Supreme Court and its chief justice, Warren Burger.

On April 26, 1978, Chief Justice Burger, in supplementing a Court ruling that extended or clarified the freedom of speech of corporations, expressed his opinion on some freedom-of-the-press issues not directly involved in the case under consideration.

First, the chief justice challenged the idea that the press had special freedoms and rights separate and distinct from those protected by the "freedom of speech" clause in the Constitution. The First Amendment, he wrote, "does not 'belong' to any definable category of persons or entities: It belongs to all who exercise its freedoms." He noted, to the consternation of some of those who hold that the press has special constitutional status, that the mention of freedom of the press, after or in addition to the mention of freedom of speech, in the Constitution really did not add much to the First Amendment. He observed, quite properly, that there was "no supporting evidence" that the men who drafted the Constitution intended, or expected, that the freedom of the press would be the basis for a special role for the institutional press.

In fact, an easy reading of the debates on the consideration of the Bill of Rights suggests that the inclusion of freedom of the press was almost incidental, or explanatory, to the freedom-of-speech clause.

Equally disturbing to the press has been the tone and the thrust of recent court decisions bearing on the actions of the press. Alan U. Schwartz, writing in the *Atlantic* of February 1977, saw danger in what he called a pendulum swing toward muzzling the press through court decisions.

Schwartz saw danger in two areas: court rulings dealing with libel and court rulings dealing with privacy. The decision on libel that disturbed Schwartz most was that made on March 2, 1976, by the Supreme Court in the case of *Time, Inc.* v. *Mary Alice Firestone,* in which Mrs. Firestone claimed *Time* had libeled her. *Time* had written that she had been divorced on grounds of extreme cruelty and adultery. She had not been found guilty of adultery.

Part of *Time*'s defense was that Mrs. Firestone was a "public person"—an argument not accepted by the Court. *Time* was referring to the Court's decision in the case of *The New York Times* v. *Sullivan* in 1964. The Court had held that a public official had to prove actual malice on the part of the press in order to win a libel action. The person bringing suit had to show "with convincing clarity" that the libel was published "with knowledge that it was false or with reckless disregard of whether it was false or not."

The theoretical justification offered (if not by the Court itself, at least by those in the press who supported and approved the decision) was that it was in the best interest of society to permit the press to criticize public officials freely without fear of being held liable for error or negligence. It was also argued that public officials were in a better position than private persons to defend themselves against falsehood and misrepresentation, although this advantage could not be actually demonstrated to exist.

In subsequent rulings (as in the case of *Rosenbloom* v. *Metromedia Inc.* in 1971), the requirement of proof of malice was extended to libel actions brought by individuals who were neither "public officials" nor "public figures," as long as the report responsible for the lawsuit involved matters of "public or general concern."

Following these rulings, the press was left free to print (without being held responsible unless malice could be proved) false statements about public figures and officials, or false statements about private citizens if the subject matter of the falsehoods carried a public interest. The press was also left free to invade both public and private citizens' privacy in such cases.

Time and changes in the personnel on the Supreme Court

brought about changes in the Court's attitude. In 1974, three years after the *Rosenbloom* decision, the Court decided in *Gertz* v. *Robert Welch, Inc.*, that it had gone too far in the earlier case. It now held that proof of malice would no longer be necessary in libel suits brought by private individuals, even though the case involved matters of public interest.

In a recent case involving action against the producer of the CBS program "60 Minutes," the Court held that the plaintiff, acknowledged to be a public figure, had a right to make inquiries on the way the program was put together to determine whether there was malice on the part of those who produced and presented it. Without proof of malice, under the *Times* v. *Sullivan* ruling, there would be little point in proceeding to prove defamation.

In a related case, one involving the invasion of privacy, the U.S. Court of Appeals for the Ninth Circuit held that unless the information that was published is "privileged as newsworthy . . . the publicizing of private facts is not protected by the First Amendment." The court sent the case back to the district court for a decision on whether the information about a Mr. Virgil, identified as a well-known body-surfer, was newsworthy. The appeals court quoted with approval a legal commentary that advised, "In determining what is a matter of legitimate public interest, account must be taken of the customs and conventions of the community; and in the last analysis, what is proper becomes a matter of the community mores." The Supreme Court refused to review the appeals court decision.

The Supreme Court has also refused to review convictions of reporters for refusing to reveal sources of information bearing on criminal trials. In his *Atlantic* article, Alan Schwartz saw the Court as having "taken a number of confused steps backward, leaving journalists, broadcasters, and publishers at the mercy of unclear laws, inconsistent judges, and subjective juries." He argued that the press should be protected and should operate in a field of almost total immunity lest it become frightened into what he called "the most far-reaching and insidious result of state censorship," namely "self-censorship." He saw the fear of libel actions and the cost of defending against libel and privacy suits as intimidating the press and as a greater threat to freedom than any laws or governmental edicts.

Schwartz seemed undisturbed that earlier court decisions left individuals at the mercy of unclear laws (for surely requiring proof of malice must leave an area of dispute that is far from clear), irresponsible journalists, eager broadcasters, and indifferent publishers, to say nothing of the arrogant ones.

Schwartz then declared a new constitutional principle, one that he says the Supreme Court fails to recognize. The principle is that "despite the undeniable value our society places on the protection of the individual from invasions of privacy and defamation, the First Amendment demands higher priority on unfettered communication. Where the two are in conflict, the latter must prevail."

Many Bill of Rights issues are not subject to clear legislative distinction and definition. The resolution of many conflicts must be in the courts, including the question of which takes precedence when two are involved. Certainly there is nothing in the arrangement or listing of the rights included in the first ten amendments that suggests an order or hierarchy, and certainly none between privacy and freedom of the press.

On this same subject, although from a slightly different point of view, Fred Shapiro, staff writer for *New Yorker* magazine, in an article in the *Washington Post* of February 6, 1977, said that the right to privacy is not spelled out anywhere in the Constitution but that the concept of the right to privacy came into being in 1888 when a federal judge,

Thomas M. Cooley, determined that a citizen had the "right to be let alone." According to Shapiro, the protection given to personal privacy, especially since the passage of the Right to Privacy Act in 1974, is interfering not only with freedom of the press but with another basic American right, not specified in the Constitution. This newly identified right, according to Shapiro, is the right "to an effective and efficient government."

Fortunately neither Schwartz nor Shapiro is on the Supreme Court.

Long before the Constitution of the United States was drafted, the British common law protected both the physical privacy of a person and the person's reputation. When the Bill of Rights was added to the Constitution, the right to privacy was taken for granted as a part of the common, colonial law. The two privacy amendments in the Bill of Rights, one protecting citizens from unreasonable search and seizure and the other against forced quartering of troops, dealt with special problems of the time.

As to the right to "efficient government" declared by Shapiro, it must be noted that nothing in the Constitution even hints at a guarantee of effective and efficient government. The Constitution was designed to provide for representative constitutional government. Self-government need not be either efficient or effective.

A spokesman for the Reporters Committee for Freedom of the Press has charged that at both federal and state governmental levels, officials are "waving the Privacy Act around" in order to keep newsmen from obtaining access to the records of agencies conducting public business and spending public money. Persons wishing to conduct academic research are making similar complaints. There are also complaints that government agencies are denying information to other government agencies.

It is possible that the privacy rules and the act are being

arbitrarily and unreasonably imposed. However, to hold that efficiency is the standard for determining when constitutional rights are to be respected would provide grounds for overriding almost every guarantee in the Bill of Rights.

Certainly, "due process" interferes with fast, efficient administration of justice, or of injustice. Freedom of religion complicates society; it makes necessary a variety of chaplain services in the armed forces. Efficiency would argue for one religion.

Colonial governments violated the privacy of their citizens and were thus more efficient in their efforts to control and suppress colonists.

Efficiency in government was one of the strong arguments made in support of the early Hitler and Mussolini political movements.

If the press had been more careful about the truth of what it printed, neither the *Firestone* nor the *Virgil* case would likely have come to trial. Neither story was a matter of great substance bearing on the public good. Rather than seek the protection of shield laws or claim special institutional privilege, the press should accept that freedom of the press is an extension of freedom of speech and acknowledge that both freedom of speech and freedom of the press are relative rights, based not on the right of anyone to say anything he wishes under any circumstances, but rather on the human need for knowledge and for truth. Since no person is sure what the truth is, the best practical way of opening the way to a knowing and understanding society is to let those who have something worth communicating (or which they think is worth communicating) say or write it, and let listeners or readers accept or reject it.

This rule of action was stated by Justice Brandeis, when he said that it is "the public's right to know," rather than the journalist's "right to publish" that is at the root of freedom of speech and of the press.

The press appears to be unmindful or unaware of its theoretical function in society, and either unmindful or indifferent to the reality of the times in which it now functions. The press today proceeds as though there were a free and competitive flow of information in this country comparable to that of 150 years ago, when there was no television or radio, and when technological limitations restricted the largest newspaper runs to about 5,000 papers a day. The reality is, in Lyndon Johnson's words to Spiro Agnew after the 1968 elections: "Young man, we have in this country two big television networks, NBC and CBS. We have two news magazines, *Newsweek* and *Time*. We have two wire services, AP and UPI. We have two pollsters, Gallup and Harris. We have two big newspapers, the *Washington Post* and the *New York Times*. They're all so damned big, they think they own the country. But, young man, don't get any ideas about fighting."

Johnson was essentially correct. Lewis H. Lapham reported in an article in *Harper's* magazine of August 1973 that "as much as ninety per cent of the news that reaches the American public arrives through the channels of the two wire services (AP and UPI), the three networks (CBS, NBC and ABC), Time Inc. (*Time, Fortune, Sports Illustrated*, etc.), the Washington Post Syndicate (which owns *Newsweek*), the New York Times Syndicate, and possibly the Knight and Newhouse newspapers."

Of course the media cannot report all of the news, but there are standards for selection which the media should recognize as guiding their profession. The press and electronic communications media do not have the right to suppress news that they do not want the public to know, especially when covering political campaigns. There are at least three standards for positive selection. Obviously, if someone is speaking sense and having an effect, there is an obligation to report what is being said. If someone is talking nonsense and having an effect, the press has, I believe, as a monopoly or near-monopoly, an obligation to report the nonsense (although it can and should challenge the nonsense with information and analysis). Consistent with this rule, the press had a responsibility to report on and cover the campaign of George Wallace.

If someone is speaking sense about current problems and not yet having any significant effect, what he says should also be reported. It is in this third area that the failure of the media is most serious. As Oswald Spengler wrote in *The Decline of the West,* "It is permitted to everyone to say what he pleases, *but* the press is free to take notice of what he says or not. It can condemn any 'truth' to death simply by not undertaking its communication to the world—a terrible censorship of silence, which is all the more potent in that the masses of newspaper readers are absolutely unaware that it exists." The danger of denial is even greater when a person becomes dependent for news, not on reading, but on one- or two-minute radio or television newscasts.

The Spengler prophecy was identified and its danger described in a recent opinion by Judge George E. MacKinnon of the U.S. Court of Appeals for the District of Columbia Circuit. The case involved the access of candidates to television audiences. Judge MacKinnon noted the argument of network lawyers who said that "a broadcaster is only required to make reasonable judgments in good faith as to the significance of a particular candidate and so decide how much time should be devoted to coverage of his campaign activities." MacKinnon then commented as follows:

> Thus, the broadcasters start by determining how significant a particular *candidate* is. If they determine that *he* is not significant, then the amount of publicity

he receives is greatly reduced—he may be effectively "frozen out" from any substantial news coverage during the entire campaign.

If the media had followed a different course and considered that the *candidate* was significant and if the media had given his campaign the same amount of coverage as it did to other candidates, his candidacy might have become of greater "significance" and the candidate might have gone on to win, or to become a serious contender.

But under present practices, as outlined by CBS, a candidate is doomed at the very beginning to having his *personal significance* as a candidate judged by the broadcasters practically before he ever starts his campaign. Thereafter the coverage of the *issues* he raises is correspondingly greatly reduced, and as a candidate he is effectively frozen out of the political campaign by the media. While the present candidates, who are appellants in this proceeding, may by general estimates be far removed from having any reasonable chance to win, the media can just as effectively, behind the screen of "news judgment," by exercising their claimed evaluation of a candidate's personal "significance," reduce its coverage of candidates who might have a chance to win, given fair coverage. And for CBS to argue that the petitioners have not "submitted any specific information to show that CBS's news judgments are unreasonable," merely compounds the error. Candidates [whom] the media freezes out from the beginning will practically never be able to demonstrate that the media's news judgments are unreasonable because they can *never* show how significant their campaigns might have become if they had received fair coverage from the beginning for the *issues* they raised. Thus, the media's early "evaluation" becomes a self-fulfilling prophecy.

The present campaign is a case in point. I venture to suggest that no person would contradict the statement that if one of the appellants received half as much coverage as the candidates of the two principal parties, his vote would be greatly increased.

The writing press in the 1976 elections followed essentially the same policy as did the broadcasters. When a Chicago newspaper columnist was asked to give some attention to our independent presidential campaign, he responded, "I don't think we can fool around; beating Ford is too important." Silence and neglect of the independent challenge that he thought might affect the outcome of the election were his chosen methods.

In much the same way, Marshall Field rejected a challenge to the neglect of the same campaign by his *Chicago Sun-Times*, saying that the country is run by a two-party system and that those candidates "chosen by the people" are the ones who deserve serious consideration. In a country with one-party politics, one can assume that press policy would be to give serious consideration to one party and its candidates "chosen by the people." In 1976, the press generally accepted subservience to two-party politics even to the point of supporting the debates that were limited to the candidates of the two major parties. The press accepted and defended the cover provided by the sponsorship of the League of Women Voters; that sponsorship exempted debates from the equal-time provisions of the Federal Communications Act by converting them into "news events." It is understandable that the networks welcomed the circumvention of the equal-time provisions of the Federal Communications Act for both commercial and political reasons, but not so easy to understand why the writing press did so. The debates were certain to become a major focus of the campaign and the influence of the writing press would be inevitably reduced to little more than passive reporting, and a kind of sportscasting pre-game and post-game commen-

tary. The only measurably significant original contributions
to the 1976 campaign from the writing press were the
Playboy interview with candidate Carter and the publicity
it received, the play given to candidate Ford's confused
statement on communism and freedom in Poland, and the
misleading headline in the *New York Daily News:* "Ford
to New York: 'Drop Dead.' " The latter was used as a basis
for a Carter television spot, with candidate Carter reassuring the people of New York that he would not tell them to
"drop dead," something Ford, of course, never said.

After the election, the press went through one of its
periods of self-examination. Some of its in-house critics
suggested that perhaps independent and third-party candidates, especially those who might have something to say
or who might have drawn votes from major candidates,
should have been given more attention. But nothing
changed. Editors felt better, and network news directors,
whose consciences are easily quieted, ceased to worry about
political coverage until the next election. As they approached 1980, they again thought of seeking exemption
from equal-time provisions. If the effort failed, they could
look forward to invitations like that of the League of
Women Voters—for a news event that would be directed by
the League and by the representatives of the candidates. The
networks might be told that they would have to use pooled
cameras and selected interviewers screened by major parties. There would be murmuring at lunch, but programming would be stopped to let the debaters get on.

The press makes fitful gestures to demonstrate fairness,
balance, or concern over its monopoly position. Many
papers have in-house critics, but there is no record that
any such critic has had a lasting effect on his paper's news
or editorial policy. This self-criticism has been described
as similar to that of a monkey at the zoo picking lice or dry

skin off its own chest. The act gives some relief but does not change the animal.

Letters to the editor and expansion of the Op-Ed pages are other offerings to fairness. Their effect in setting up balance in the press or an adversary presentation is minimal. Along with serious articles, Op-Ed pages usually carry others that are on the edge of the ridiculous, if not over the edge. The seriousness of the Op-Ed page is reflected in its treatment by the *New York Times*. The *Times,* by long tradition, has not carried cartoons on its editorial page. The explanation has been that it judges cartoons to be a distraction from the serious thought being presented in its editorials. On its Op-Ed page, however, the *Times* regularly carries distracting cartoons—pictures of men on horseback with trees growing out of their heads, and the like. Evidently, distraction on the Op-Ed page is not a serious concern to the *Times* editors. It does serve as a marked contrast with the seriousness of the left-hand editorial page (the official, approved commentary) for which the editors take full responsibility.

The press seems unaware of the relationship and interdependence of all of the freedoms guaranteed by the Bill of Rights, and often gives the impression (if it does not quite assert) that as long as there is freedom of the press, all other freedoms and liberties will be secure. Any person, profession, or institution protected by the Constitution has a very special responsibility to be concerned about the protection of the rights guaranteed to others. Churches, for example, which enjoy the protection guaranteed by the freedom of religion, cannot safely advocate restrictions of others' rights without endangering their own freedom. A political party protected by freedom of assembly should not interfere with freedom of others to organize. It should not interfere with the freedom of speech or with freedom of the press unless it wishes to run the risk of endangering its own security. Nor can the press, for the sake of its own freedom, safely be indifferent to interference with freedom of speech or assembly, or the right of privacy or due process, or any other freedoms guaranteed by the Constitution.

But the press has been indifferent and careless. When the Supreme Court, in 1976, held that the Federal Election Campaign Act violated freedom of speech in provisions which had generally been supported by the press, the press did not report the Court decision as a victory for freedom of speech. (Freedom of the press was not threatened by this act.) Instead they described the decision (which held that no monetary limit could be placed on expenditures of personal funds by anyone to advance political ideas) with the headline "Fat Cats Protected by Supreme Court."

Failure of the writing press, or what is called the "print media," to understand and meet its responsibilities is especially serious, for it is through the writing press that lines of thought and policy are developed on which reasoned judgment can be passed.

The writing press is not under technological pressure or the pressure of time to present a story and provide instant analysis within one or two minutes, nor are newspapers in danger of losing licenses, as are television and radio stations.

The profession of journalism is not an easy one. It must be exercised under criticism, even under threat. Winston Churchill said of democracy that it is the worst form of government, except for the other forms that have been tried from time to time. So one can, even must, say the same of a "free press."

Federal Communications Commission

Let there be two political parties, and no more

According to some studies, the American people get 80 percent of their news from television reports. How their ideas about culture, art, and religion are affected, if not formed, by television has not yet been determined. Measurements would be helpful, but even without them it is possible to see the potential of the Federal Communications Commission as a bureaucratic center for the control and direction of culture, of news, of political communications, of advertising, of entertainment, of popular education.

The beginnings of this government agency were modest. The Communications Act of 1934 established the Federal Communications Commission with powers to regulate radio, powers later extended to cover television.

The principle underlying the laws controlling radio and television is that the granting of the license is, in effect, a grant of a monopolistic right by society, which acknowledges the obvious fact that listeners and viewers do not have the power of selection over radio and television that they have in subscribing to newspapers or in the reading of the printed word.

Observers of television in its later stages have described this condition of dependency in more disturbing ways. Marshall McLuhan, for example, noted that television caused the medium to become its own message. Nicholas Johnson, a former member of the Federal Communications Commission, said that television is a means of communication suitable only for the totalitarian state, where control of news and the conditioning of the people are accepted in theory and in practice.

Fundamental to the view that the electronic media should be socially controlled is its monopolistic character. As protection and defense against controlled communication, the "fairness doctrine" holds that all significant points of view must be presented by radio and television stations. This doctrine was set forth in a Federal Communications Commission report published in 1949. In that report, the commission stated that the "doctrine" imposes two responsibilities on broadcasters: coverage of issues of public importance must be adequate and it must fairly reflect differing viewpoints. The language of the report followed the language of a 1945 Supreme Court decision involving the Associated Press, which included these words: "Surely a command [the First Amendment guarantee of freedom of speech and of the press] that the government itself shall not impede the free flow of ideas does not afford nongovernmental combinations a refuge if they impose restraints upon that constitutionally guaranteed freedom."

Twenty years later, the Supreme Court, in *Red Lion Broadcasting Company* v. *FCC*, refined the theory of fairness and the relationship of the broadcasting industry to the First Amendment.

First the Court sustained the government's right to license broadcasting stations and observed further that the First Amendment did not confer upon anyone the right to operate a broadcasting station. The Court further affirmed that in licensing and operating radio and television stations it is "the right of the viewers and listeners, not the right of the broadcasters, which is paramount."

And, said the Court, "as far as the First Amendment is concerned, those who are licensed stand no better than those to whom licenses are refused. A license permits broadcasting, but the licensee has no constitutional right to be the one who holds the license or to monopolize a radio frequency to the exclusion of his fellow citizens. There is nothing in the First Amendment which prevents the government from requiring a licensee to share his frequency with others and to conduct himself as a proxy or fiduciary with obligations to present those views and voices which are representative of his community and which would otherwise, by necessity, be barred from the airwaves."

The difference of note between the writing press and the electronic media was the scarcity factor, i.e., the limited number of available radio and television broadcasting frequencies.

The fairness doctrine requires two basic responses from broadcasting companies: first, that adequate time be provided for the discussion of public issues, and second, that there be reasonable opportunity given for the presentation of opposing viewpoints. Within the range of these broad rules, the owners or directors of radio and television stations and networks have been allowed great discretion and are only rarely called to account before either the FCC or the courts.

FCC rulings relative to the fairness doctrine have seldom been successfully challenged by any political group or organization other than the Republicans and Democrats. In a case known as the Zapple case (May 6, 1970), the FCC held that if a station sold time to one candidate so that he could present his case to the public, it would have to give his opponents the right to buy the same amount of time in which to respond. However, the commission explained that the policy applied only to major political parties. Under this interpretation of the fairness doctrine, a

Socialist party candidate who had been attacked by Republicans and Democrats would not have the right to buy time in which to answer their charges.

Whereas the fairness doctrine obviously was intended to apply generally, it has been and continues to be interpreted by the FCC and by the courts as applying only to Republicans and Democrats. Rulings reflect immediate political pressures rather than law or precedent.

Section 315 of the Communications Act of 1934 provides that a licensee who provides time to a legally qualified candidate for any public office must "afford equal opportunities" to all other candidates for the same office. Commonly called the "equal-time requirement," this used to protect minority-party and independent candidates. In 1959, however, Congress amended the law to exempt newscasts, news interviews, and political conventions from the equal-time requirement.

The truly national test of the equal-time requirement occurred in 1960, when debates between candidates John Kennedy and Richard Nixon were proposed. The interested parties—the candidates and their committees, and the radio and television broadcasters—accepted that the equal-time provision would apply to the debates, and that unless Section 315 of the law were suspended, candidates of minority parties would have to be offered comparable time and exposure. Consequently, the Congress suspended Section 315, and the debates took place.

The action might have been challenged in court under First Amendment rights by candidates other than those of the two major parties, but it was not. In any case the action was orderly and legal. Obviously, all parties involved thought the debates, scheduled and programmed as they were, could not be considered as bona fide news events, despite the liberalization and expansion of that definition in the 1959 revision of the Communications Act of 1934.

The next serious test of equal opportunity and fairness came in 1964, shortly before the November election. In late October, President Johnson, who was then running against Senator Barry Goldwater, the Republican candidate for the presidency, announced a major presidential address.

The networks were hesitant about covering it as though it were a public event and reportedly gave some thought to reporting it as an ordinary news story, including parts of it in their regular newscasts. Political considerations prevailed. The networks carried the speech live as a special news event. The fact that the networks anticipated that President Johnson would be reelected by an overwhelming majority may have played some part in the decision to cover the speech live and in its entirety.

Twelve years later, in 1976, again shortly before the November election, President Ford announced a press conference. Again, the networks deliberated as to whether the appearance of the President should be covered live and in its entirety, or reported as a part of their regular newscasts. There were exceptions, but most broadcasters treated the Ford appearance not as a presidential news conference, but as ordinary news.

One network spokesman said that the decision reflected what he termed "the nearness doctrine," namely the nearness of the press conference to the election. This doctrine had not been recognized in 1964. The spokesman might have been more accurate if he had announced a new doctrine of "closeness," in the anticipated results of the election. The polls at the time the "nearness doctrine" was announced showed that candidate Carter might well win. It was reasonable to suppose that a newly elected President whose opponent had been given fifteen minutes to a half-hour of free network time within a few days of the election might have been less than friendly to the electronic media who had been so generous to his opponent.

The substance of the 1964 Johnson speech, which the media covered, was his view of what he termed an important change in the leadership of the Russian government, plus his views on an explosion of a nuclear device by the Communist Chinese.

When the Republicans asked for equal time, the FCC held that there had been no violations of the fairness doctrine in the broadcasting of the Johnson speech. The commission cited as precedent a ruling given to the three major networks in 1956, when the networks asked if they could, without violating the law, broadcast a fifteen-minute report to the nation by President Eisenhower on the Suez crisis. Obviously that event was a genuine crisis requiring policy decisions on the part of the United States, a wholly different matter from the Johnson speech.

Denial of time to the Republicans was upheld by a divided circuit court in the District of Columbia in a decision that was denied review when it was appealed to the Supreme Court. Justice Arthur Goldberg and Justice Hugo Black dissented.

Justice Goldberg, in the dissent, said the question raised by the Republican petition was substantial and warranted argument, which, in view of the imminence of the election, should be set immediately if the petitioner was to be given any practical relief.

He cited Section 315 of the Federal Communications Act: "If any licensee shall permit any person who is a legally qualified candidate for any public office to use a broadcasting station, he shall afford equal opportunities to all other such candidates for that office in the use of such broadcasting station: Provided that such licensee shall have no power of censorship over the material broadcast under the provisions of this section."

The justice went on to point out that "the statute on its face plainly requires that a licensee who permits any legally qualified candidate for any public office to use its broadcast facilities afford equal opportunities to all other qualified candidates. No exemption is made for a legally qualified candidate who is the incumbent President of the United States."

The justice continued, "The express exceptions to the broad scope of the statute for bona fide broadcasts, news interviews, news documentaries and on-the-spot coverage of bona fide news events do not appear to apply to the address made by the President on Sunday, October 18, 1964, which does not seem to fit into any of these categories."

The justice was right. The FCC had moved beyond denying the protection of the "fairness doctrine" to third-party candidates to denying equal time to a major-party candidate who was not likely to defeat an incumbent of the other major party.

Nineteen seventy-six promised to be a difficult year for the radio and television broadcasters, since it appeared almost certain that the Democrats would control Congress, but the outcome of the presidential election was in doubt. It was the better part of wisdom for the media to try to keep both parties happy.

Networks or their spokespersons approached Congress proposing a suspension of the equal-time provisions of the law, not for public debate as was the purpose in 1960, for public debates had not yet been proposed, but so that the radio-television industry could give Republicans and Democrats equal time without being obliged by law to give it to any other parties or to their candidates.

Congress did not respond with any enthusiasm, believing that the 1959 amendments to the Communications Act had broadened the exemptions from the equal-time provisions of the original law sufficiently. Moreover, in the years following the 1959 changes in the law, radio and television stations had carefully included fringe candidates in programs like "Meet the Press," "Face the Nation," and "Issues and Answers" and had generally avoided charges of discrimination. They had also adopted the practice of giving the party not in control of the presidency time to respond following the broadcast of presidential messages.

All might have gone well, with the radio and television broadcasters being careful to honor the equal-time and fairness doctrines as they applied to Republicans and Democrats and ignoring or rejecting the complaints of third-party and independent candidates, if the proposal for debates between the presidential candidates of the two major parties had not been made.

The 1959 amendments to the Federal Communications Act had clearly not exempted "staged debates." Once the debates were proposed, the problem of getting around the equal-time provisions of the law became of critical importance. Since Congress had failed to change the law, a new approach to avoid or circumvent the restrictive provisions had been developed.

The idea of presidential debates did not come by chance, or by sudden inspiration or vision, to the president of the League of Women Voters, which later sponsored them. The debates of 1976 were, in fact, the end product of eighteen months of planning, political maneuvering, and possibly some conspiracy. The idea and the action began in 1975 with the Aspen Institute of Humanistic Studies, which has its headquarters in Aspen, Colorado. The president of Atlantic Richfield Oil Company is chairman of the Aspen Institute.

In March 1975, Douglass Cater, head of the institute's Program on Communications and Society, convened a round-table conference in Aspen's Washington office. In attendance were thirty-one representatives from political parties, the broadcasting industry, candidates, government, and public-interest groups.

Among the participants were Lawrence Secrest, chief assistant to the then FCC chairman Richard Wiley; Nicholas Zapple, aide to then Senator John Pastore, who had taken a special interest in the FCC and laws controlling communications (in 1975 Pastore was chairman of the Senate Subcommittee on Communications); Robert Strauss, then chairman of the Democratic National Committee; Sig Mickelson, former president of CBS News (and with the Medill School of Journalism in 1975); and Henry Geller, former general counsel to the FCC and later to be assistant secretary of commerce for communications and information in the Carter administration. The Republican National Committee, the *Washington Post* broadcast stations, Common Cause, and the League of Women Voters were also represented.

From this conference began the effort that climaxed in the debates between Ford and Carter, in prime time on all three commercial networks and on public television, with all other candidates and parties denied participation or comparable television and radio time.

The pointed and practical concern of the conference was the elimination or circumvention of the equal-time provisions of the Communications Act, so that, as the conferees said, the bicentennial would be a "model political broadcast year" (whatever that is).

Sig Mickelson came prepared with a paper outlining options available to the group. Most desirable, he thought, was the simple repeal of Section 315 of the Communications Act of 1934, the section that contains the equal-time provisions. Participants concluded that there was little hope that Congress would take that action. A second line of attack was suggested by a conference participant and later prepared by Henry Geller, who argued for a direct attack on the FCC's ruling of the previous thirteen years. Geller charged that the rulings on political debates since 1962 had been in error and recommended a clear about-face, something rare in federal agencies acting without congressional or presidential assurance or encouragement.

Geller gave his brief to Douglass Cater, who, acting for the Aspen Institute, submitted it for judgment to the FCC, thus beginning what has become known as the Aspen Case. It was an unusual case in that there was no real complainant, no offended candidate or party, but only the Aspen Institute asking for a new interpretation of the law.

The chairman of the FCC, Richard Wiley, seemed unsurprised by the Geller brief and quite ready to take it up for consideration. The Geller proposition offered the best of two worlds to the broadcasters. They could escape the limitations of the equal-time provisions of the law when they wished to in order to protect themselves politically, yet they could invoke the equal-time provisions in the interest of service to the two major parties, or for reasons of profit, when they wished to.

The Aspen petition did not get lost in bureaucratic channels. The normal rule-making process is for the commission to post public notice and invite public comment. No such public notice was given in this instance. Why it was not, in a case of such obvious public interest and concern, has not been satisfactorily explained.

Even before the FCC had cast its official vote on the Aspen Case, Chairman Wiley, in a September 16, 1975, speech to the International Radio and Television Society, announced that the commission would soon rule that presidential debates were to be exempt from equal-time rules. There was great applause from the assembly. While it is common for the FCC and other commissions to inform concerned parties of action up for consideration, it is rare that commissions announce future actions before formal procedures have been carried out. In this case, the public announcement was made before many who might have opposed the change could voice their opposition.

The commission vote on the Aspen case, on September 25, 1975, was not unanimous. Commissioners Robert E. Lee and Benjamin L. Hooks dissented. Lee, a longtime member of the commission, held that the change being proposed was clearly the prerogative of Congress. "During my tenure at the Commission," he wrote, "we have repeatedly told Congress that we are responsible for communications matters, not political decisions." Hooks, the only independent on the commission (and now head of the NAACP), wrote, "The majority may no longer be pleased with the journalistic strictures set forth in Sec. 315(a) but we cannot legally strain to interpret that statute so as to annul congressional acts."

So the FCC ruled that debates between presidential candidates were exempt from the equal-time provisions of the Communications Act. However, the FCC had held that the debates, in order to be exempt, must be sponsored by a neutral party, not the candidates or the networks or other broadcasters. Why the candidates should be excluded is difficult to understand. Under this ruling, the Lincoln-Douglas debates would not have qualified. If this ruling were applied to boxing, a fight arranged by fighters or their managers might be judged not to be a news event, and therefore not to be covered without the sponsorship of a third or neutral party.

The "neutral sponsorship" obstacle was not a serious one for those set on avoiding the restraints of the equal-time provisions of the law. The way to avoidance had already been prepared by Charles Benton of Wilmette, Illinois, a financial supporter of the Aspen Institute. In the summer of 1975, James Karayn, president of the National Public Affairs Center for Broadcasting, was hired by Benton to map out details for a series of Presidential Forums or joint appearances of presidential candidates during the primaries. Karayn is credited with having thought of the League of

Women Voters as sponsor because, as he said, it had an "impeccable record of nonpartisanship." The word should have been "bipartisanship."

Benton asked Karayn to put what was required (by way of detachment and neutrality) into writing. Then Benton gave the League a call. The League accepted responsibility for sponsorship. Karayn was then hired to direct the League's Presidential Forums, on which candidates in Democratic primaries appeared. (The Republican candidates declined to appear.) The forums were supported by $200,000 contributed by the William Benton Foundation. Karayn then moved on to direct the League's presidential-debate-sponsoring activities.

The debate steering committee included among its members Charles Benton, Douglass Cater, James Karayn, representatives of the Democratic and Republican parties, former FCC chairman Newton Minow, and Rita Hauser, who in 1972 had served as a co-chairperson of Nixon's Committee to Re-elect the President. Testifying before the Senate Subcommittee on Communications, Ms. Hauser set the tone when she said that "the line has to be drawn somewhere. This is a two-party country, and one of those two is going to be elected." When and how the League decided that this is to be a two-party country has never been clear.

The matter of neutral sponsorship having been taken care of, the debate promoters faced the more tricky challenge of avoiding involvement of candidates and broadcasters in the arrangement of the news events. The League, evidently with the best intentions, was a willing instrument for Benton and Karayn.

The high point of League participation was in its dictating to the camera crews where cameras were to be placed and denying the cameramen the right to film the studio audience. This caused Richard Salant, then head of news at CBS, to protest that freedom of the press was being abused and to threaten to withdraw the coverage by his network. Then he walked out of the meeting, only to overcome his professional scruples and have CBS join the other networks and the Public Broadcasting Service in decent subordination to political and economic pressure.

The League moved further to control the debates. It picked moderators and the panel of journalists for the debates, after consultation with (some say approval by) the participants.

The League issued the invitations to Ford and Carter, saying that if anyone else were included, all the other ninety-odd presidential candidates would have to be included. No one from the League ever explained how the League could limit the debate to two, but not to three, without including all the other candidates.

When asked how the League would respond to those who suggested that the League was a front for the debates, League director Peggy Lampl said simply, "We call them sexist."

Whereas I and my committee, as well as other candidates and their supporters, believed that, even without the scheduled debates, the equal-time and fairness doctrines were being violated daily by both radio and television stations and the networks, we thought it pointless to go to the Federal Communications Commission for relief. All members of the commission except one were either Republicans or Democrats. It was the same commission that, with only two dissents, had already ruled in the Aspen case that debates were, if properly sponsored, exempt from the equal-time provisions of the law. In September 1976 we attempted to get our case directly before the courts, in this case the U.S. District Court of the District of Columbia. Our lawyers, led by John Armor, asked the court to grant both declaratory and injunctive relief by requiring the League of Women Voters and the television and radio media who were cooperating with the League to include me in the debates if they were to be held, or to stop the debates.

Our basic argument was that by any reasonable standards I should be considered a major candidate, unless that term was to be applied only to Democrats and Republicans. Our lawyers argued that if major candidates could only be Republicans or Democrats, the Constitution would be violated. By its narrow interpretation of the meaning of "major candidates," the FCC was in fact giving Republicans and Democrats privileged treatment.

There was no clear statutory definition of a "major candidate" in the Federal Election Campaign Act, which became fully operational for the first time in 1976. It did set forth some conditions, discussed elsewhere in this book, concerning funds already raised, which distinguished some candidates from others, although it did not distinguish between "major" and "minor" ones.

There were several limiting conditions in the law, all directed toward eliminating nonserious candidates. For example, a candidate had to show continuing strength in primaries (10 percent of the vote in two successive primaries) and also evidence of popular support.

At the time we filed our petition for injunctive relief, only three candidates, Carter, Ford, and myself, met three basic tests of being on the ballot in twenty or more states, being on the ballot in enough states to win a majority in the electoral college, and receiving more than 5 percent in the polls.

We pointed out, in support of our petition, that only four other third-party or independent presidential candidates had met these three qualifications in the twentieth century: George Wallace in 1968, Henry Wallace in 1948, Robert La Follette in 1924, and Theodore Roosevelt in 1912.

We argued that unless the term "major candidates" meant only Republicans and Democrats, I should be included in the debate and given the same treatment, under the "equal time" or "equal opportunity" provisions of the Communications Act, as was being given to Ford and Carter.

This argument would work only if the court found that the debates were not bona fide news events and therefore were subject to the equal-time provisions of the law.

We made a second argument in support of the injunction on the fairness doctrine of the Federal Communications Act. Our lawyers argued that excluding me from the debates was a judgment on me and a statement by sponsors of the debates that my candidacy was not a "serious" one, that a vote for me would be wasted, and that the positions I was presenting on critical issues were not to be taken seriously; the exclusion from the debates was, in itself, an attack on my candidacy.

Further, we urged that I be included in the debates on the grounds that even though equal time (quantitatively measured) might be given to me at another time, it would not be truly equal, since the debates were a unique event. The case cited in support of this contention was *Brown* v. *Board of Education* (1954), in which the Supreme Court held that "in the field of public education, the doctrine of 'separate but equal' has no place. Separate educational facilities are inherently unequal."

The district court, for a number of reasons, including legal, technical ones, refused to give us the relief we requested and directed us to take our case through regular channels, including an appeal to the Federal Communications Commission.

We complied, although we expected little or no support from the commission that was so closely involved in the arrangements for the two-party debates. Procedurally, the situation was that if the FCC rejected our case, we could then appeal directly to the Court of Appeals for the District of Columbia Circuit, and, beyond that, to the Supreme Court.

Dutifully we reported to the FCC much of what they already knew. We said that officers of the League of Women Voters had decided to sponsor (if permitted) debates between candidates for the presidency of the United States. On or about June 15, 1976, the League formed a committee headed by Newton Minow, former chairman of the FCC, to organize the debates; and just prior to the Democratic National Convention, the League contacted representatives of candidate Carter and were told that he might be willing to participate, but only if the participants were himself and Ford, and no others. (At the time, the Harris Poll showed that I had a potential 10 percent of the vote nationally, of which 87 percent would have been drawn from Carter.)

We said further that just before the Republican National Convention the League contacted both Ford and Reagan about taking part in the debates and were informed that both were willing to, if nominated, but only if their opponent was Jimmy Carter. All the networks informed the League that they would carry the debates live, in full, on prime time as a news story, but that the League would have to bear the costs of the local telecasts. The League then discovered that neither the Democratic nor the Republican presidential candidate would pay any costs of the debates. The League then contacted the Federal Election Commission, requesting a ruling that would permit donations to the League to pay expenses.

On August 30, 1976, the FEC issued a ruling allowing such donations. Having received notice, through a leak, that Carter intended to challenge him to debate, Ford anticipated the challenge in his speech accepting the Republican presidential nomination, by challenging Carter. Carter accepted the next morning. All the conditions for the "news event" were then settled.

I immediately requested the League of Women Voters to include me in the debates. The League never replied directly, but, in a statement to a *New York Times* reporter early in September, said that I would not be invited to participate in their news event. Later a League official wrote me that her organization was "considering a fifth debate for those presidential candidates who are on the ballot in a substantial number of states . . . As soon as our plans with respect to such a debate are firmer we will, of course, be in touch with you." That was the last we heard from the League.

The Federal Communications Commission, having previously issued a memorandum that equal-time provisions of the law did not apply to presidential debates, on October 5 ruled against us by a vote of four to one.

All Republican and Democratic members of the commission who participated in the decision voted to restrict the debates to the Republican and Democratic candidates. The only dissenting vote was from the independent member of the commission, Benjamin Hooks.

Hooks, in his dissent, made this case against the action of the majority of the commission:

> I do not blame the League of Women Voters which, in order to fit the cracked mold for a debate exemption from 47 U.S.C. §315(a)(4) devised by the Commission in its *Aspen Institute* ruling, has had to engage in all manner of subterfuge and charade to make it appear that the current Presidential polemics are autonomous news events rather than the premeditated media extravaganza they clearly are to everyone still enjoying the blessings of earthly life.
>
> We are all victims—the League, the candidates, the

voters, the media—of the *Aspen* ruling which makes everyone *pretend* that these debates are a spontaneous occurrence (like a forest fire) or a routinely scheduled newsworthy event (like the Super Bowl) which would have occurred anyway, with or without the conspired presence of the media. The world-at-large is not fooled into believing that these debates would have taken place without the direct involvement and commitment of the networks. However, like Shakespeare, the FCC by this action affirms that "(t)he play's the thing." . . .

Accordingly, I dissent. In so doing, I reiterate that I do not necessarily blame the League or the media. Moreover, had the Congress suspended §315 and the networks been allowed to come out of the closet as the true superintendents, the complaint of the National Newspaper Publishers Association about the absence of Black correspondents might have been unnecessary. I would hope that the networks would have been more sensitive to, and would have avoided, the all-white correspondent panels of the first two debates, thereby assuring that questions in the minds of millions of minority citizens would have been asked of the candidates.

We were pleased with the Hooks dissent and hoped the federal appeals court in the District would give us a full hearing, and even a favorable ruling. The court had on it a number of members who had clear records in support of the basic guarantees of the Bill of Rights, a factor we hoped would outweigh the fact that all members were identified with either the Republican or the Democratic party, and each might hope to move to the Supreme Court. Such a move would require that the justice be nominated by a Republican or Democratic President and approved by a Senate made up (with the current exception of Senator Harry Byrd, who was elected as an independent) of Republicans and Democrats.

The first debate had been held on September 23, 1976. Our complaint, which the district court had rejected, was filed with the FCC on September 24. The commission ruled against us on October 5. We immediately took our case to the appeals court, hoping to have a decision before the third debate, which was scheduled for October 22, 1976.

The arguments made to the appeals court were essentially the same ones we had made at the district court level and to the Federal Communications Commission. By this time, I was the only candidate seeking relief. The other candidates, Tom Anderson of the American party, Lester Maddox of the American Independent party, and Peter Camejo of the Socialist Workers party, were no longer seeking further legal remedies for discrimination against them. We argued that my candidacy was the only one that had continued to gain support, and that it was recognized as one that could well affect the outcome of the election.

Noting that a 5 percent figure was accepted in the Federal Election Campaign Act as the percentage of the vote that would make an independent or third-party candidate eligible for a percentage share in federal campaign funds (although only after the election), we argued that I was deserving of consideration different from other candidates (generally referred to as "fringe" candidates), since I was the only one other than Ford and Carter showing strength above 5 percent in the national polls. At the time of our filing our case before the appeals court, we said that every poll taken by Harris, Gallup, Yankelovich, CBS, the *New York Times*, and by the Republicans and the Democrats, with but one exception, showed my candidacy with more than 5 percent support.

The three major networks, joined by the Public Broadcasting Service, all entered briefs supporting the FCC and opposing our complaint. With minor differences of text and emphasis, all four briefs could have been written in the same office by the same lawyer or lawyers. This was not too surprising, for over the years the three major networks have come to think almost identically on matters involving possible conflict with the Republican and Democratic parties. Without conferring, without collusion, without conspiracy, they come up with the same decisions to grant equal time to Democrats in order to answer speeches by Republican Presidents, even when there is no question of fairness or equal opportunity involved, and to do the same for Republicans when Democratic Presidents speak.

The networks dismissed our claims under the equal-time doctrine by sustaining the commission's ruling that the debates were news events. Of course if that ruling was accepted, they were quite right. But we argued that the evidence was clear that the debates were contrived and controlled in part by the networks, who were reported to have said they would cover them only if the participants were Carter and Ford.

Spokesmen for the networks and also for the FCC took great pains to defend against the least serious charge made by our lawyers: the argument that the fact that the participants in the debate remained silent and almost immobile during the twenty-eight minutes of sound failure that interrupted the first debate demonstrated that the debates were staged and controlled, and therefore not bona fide news events. Following this debate we had asked for equal time —forty-five minutes of air time with sound (the amount of time used by each of the candidates with sound) and fourteen minutes without sound, half of the twenty-eight minutes during which Carter and Ford were exposed to public view without saying or doing anything that was observable. I argued mildly with the lawyers over making the point, since I thought that the period without sound was the only noncontrolled, nonstaged part of the joint appearance and that the twenty-eight minutes and the reaction, or nonreaction, of the candidates was the only bona fide news event of the whole performance.

There was a point, however, to our lawyers' argument. It is unlikely that if there had been a camera failure during the time that ABC was filming its exclusive of the Indianapolis 500, the race would have been delayed for twenty-eight minutes to allow for correction of technical difficulties.

It is possible that the projected invasion of Haiti, to which a CBS operative had bought the television rights with the knowledge that the advance would provide money to help finance the revolution, might have been turned on and off while the cameras were adjusted and moved to better locations. It is also possible that camera crews from other networks might have been denied the right to televise the action, as CBS and NBC were excluded from covering the Indianapolis 500 by virtue of the ABC contract. At best they might have been allowed to take what came through to them from the CBS operations, as CBS, NBC, and PBS accepted the ABC technicians, acting under the direction of the League of Women Voters, on the first presidential debate. We argued that the debates created a unique situation that could not be duplicated, and that the only way to meet the requirements and purposes of the law was that I participate with the other two candidates. We based our argument on one the television stations themselves made. It was not just any time we were asking for, but the kind of time that CBS had defined when my committee tried to buy the half-hour scheduled for the program "Maude." CBS told us they could not sell us "Maude"'s time without violating, in an absolute, even metaphysical way, the equal-time provisions of the Federal Communications Act. For, CBS said, "Maude"'s time is unique (marked eternally, one could conclude). If they sold it to us, no other candidate could ever be given equal time, through all the ages of the world. It was a compelling argument.

We thought of going to court, as other candidates had done when denied the right to buy time. Since the other cases did not involve "unique time," we decided against bringing the case.

Radio and television have developed new conceptions of time and new measurements. For the first time in history, time has been offered for sale. (Space had been sold and the effects of time had been postponed, as in *Faust* and *The Picture of Dorian Gray,* but never time itself.)

If time were to be offered for sale, it had to be graded. Time came to be classified "prime," "choice," and "good," just like beef. The classifications for cattle continue down through "common," "canner," and "cutter," and these names could also, with a little imagination, be applied to the time allowed for television programs.

Time is not easy to handle. Philosophers, theologians, poets, watchmakers all have tried, without success, to comprehend it. Failing that, they have tried to control it through definition or measurement.

It was the commission's ruling concerning the fairness doctrine and the debates which we thought the court might be most ready to overturn. The commission had acknowledged that broadcasters who present a discussion on one side of a controversial issue of public importance "must afford a reasonable opportunity for the presentation of contrasting points of view" in their overall programming. Ordinarily the broadcaster decides how best to present the contrasting viewpoints, with his decisions subject to review by the FCC. The commission then stated that in order to promote political discussion of issues, "the commission must be able to assure the broadcaster that his decisions as to the significance of particular candidates and the amount of coverage to be devoted to the campaigns of the candidates will not be disturbed [without] a *prima facie* showing by a complainant that these decisions were un- reasonable or were made in bad faith." The commission held that we had not made a showing on either of these two points.

Of course we had never argued bad faith on the part of broadcasters. Rather we pointed out their nearly auto- matic, unreflective readiness to limit debate to the two political parties on which the broadcasters depend for continuation of licenses.

We also argued that my exclusion from the debates as well as the small amount of time given generally by the broadcasters to the positions I was taking on critical issues, along with the recognized fact that the vote I might get could well determine the outcome of the election, did con- stitute a case under the fairness doctrine.

The most ludicrous argument made against our appeal was the claim that giving relief to me would interfere with the freedom-of-speech rights of the networks, their employ- ees, and Ford and Carter.

This is Orwellian, *1984* logic, for the essence of the argument was that if I or my case were given more tele- vision time, there would be less time for Ford and Carter and for broadcast employees, and that consequently their freedom of speech would be interfered with. Earlier in the campaign, broadcasters had refused to sell time to the Libertarian candidate, Roger MacBride, until the Republi- can and the Democratic conventions were over, on the grounds that to do so would give him an advantage before the major parties had chosen their candidates. In other words, MacBride's freedom of speech came into effect only after the Republicans and the Democrats had picked their presidential candidates. This too is a strange interpretation of freedom of speech and of the equal-time provisions of the Communications Act.

In response to our arguments under the fairness doctrine, CBS said that their coverage of my campaign reflected their professional judgment as to the relative significance of my candidacy. They pointed out the "extended interview" with me on the CBS morning news on September 22, 1976, and my inclusion on the "CBS Evening News with Walter Cronkite" on August 23 and again on August 30. They also cited an interview with me on September 17 in a news documentary, "Campaign '76," and another interview on October 3 on "Face the Nation."

The CBS position was similar to that of NBC when they opposed our complaint to the FCC. NBC told the commissioners that my candidacy was not sufficiently significant to deserve significant coverage, and then went on to say that even were I entitled "to coverage of some sort, there is no showing that NBC's coverage did not satisfy that obligation." NBC reported that I was included in their Saturday news on August 28, that I was mentioned by Floyd Kalber on the "Today Show" on August 30 and again by Irving R. Levine on the "Today Show" on August 31, and that I was interviewed on the "Today Show" of September 1.

This coverage in a five-day period was all related to our complaint against the debates and showed no reporting of my position on the substantial issues in the campaign. NBC further argued that their failure to cover my campaign was justified by national polls. They then cited the Harris Poll (September 23–25), the NBC Poll (September 16–17), and the Gallup Poll (August 6) and observed that while none of these polls gave me more than 8 percent of the vote, President Ford's and Governor Carter's support varied between 33 and 52 percent of the vote.

NBC did not indicate what showing in the polls would

have been considered significant by their experts. If the polls gave me between 5 and 8 percent, I should have been getting roughly one-fourth to one-sixth as much coverage as was being given to Ford and Carter in this period.

An ABC brief was the most irrelevant of those filed by the major networks. These statements are typical: "It is clear that McCarthy has totally misconceived both the design and function of the fairness doctrine. That policy seeks to promote informative broadcasting by requiring that licensees provide a balanced treatment of controversial issues of public importance in their overall programming. The doctrine relates to issues, not *individuals*." And: "In the political election context, the policy underlying the fairness doctrine is to foster a fair presentation of numerous viewpoints on important political issues, not to mandate specific exposure for any particular candidate."

Our charge was that my position was not being presented, and that the best way to present it was through reporting my campaign in the same way that the networks were reporting on the Ford and Carter campaigns. There were at least four issues important to the country on which I differed from Ford and Carter. They were energy, inflation, militarism and arms production, and the undermining of open and free politics through the passage of the Federal Election Campaign Act. On a fifth issue, tax policy, I was also in disagreement with both Ford and Carter, although these differences were not as sharp as my disagreement on the other four issues. Each issue should have been considered by the voters of the country in the 1976 election. But in the judgment of those who control television news, none was judged important enough.

I said that the nation had to change its wasteful habits of overconsumption, especially of fuel, and more particularly curb the excessive waste caused by oversized, overweight, and overpowered cars. Our estimate was that as much as

$100 billion of the approximately $400 billion spent each year in support of automobile transportation could be saved without requiring any significant shift or change in the everyday lives of Americans. At the same time candidate Carter was talking generalities about the energy problem and the need for conservation, while candidate Ford was encouraging the production of more domestic fuel. In April 1977, six months after his election, President Carter discovered the seriousness of the energy problem and announced the existence of a "crisis."

On the matter of employment, I argued that the only way structural unemployment in America could be reduced was through a redistribution of existing work, and recommended a shortened work day, week, year, or lifetime, urging a shorter work year as the best method. Despite forty years of technological advance, we cling to the work rules adopted in the late thirties and early forties, when the eight-hour day, the five-day week, and the fifty-week working year became standard. The Carter-Ford debate on unemployment had been reduced to a no-decision argument over the relationship of inflation to unemployment; its high point came when the sound system failed, and its low point in the claims and counterclaims by each as to which of them, as President, would provide more public-service jobs.

While the Ford and Carter debate on inflation went round and round on the issues of imposing wage-price controls versus voluntary controls and whether interest rates were too high, I proposed standby wage and price controls for the major noncompetitive industries and selective controls to direct credit to those areas in the economy where it was most necessary, and away from those in which the greatest inflationary pressures were operating. I also proposed that tax provisions such as investment credit, accelerated depreciation, and excise taxes be changed to make it possible for persons whose income was principally from wages and salaries to save and invest, and recommended a tax change to allow retention of capital gains on home sales.

The defense arguments between Ford and Carter were, at most, superficial. Ford said that he favored producing the B-1 bomber. Carter said he wasn't sure whether he would produce it or not. Carter charged that the National Guard units in the United States were not adequately armed. Ford said that they were adequately armed.

Issues such as the possible manufacture and deployment of cruise missiles, construction of additional Trident submarines, and the manufacture of the neutron bomb were never debated. None of these issues was considered of enough substantive merit to warrant their being publicized by the broadcasters during the campaign.

The Public Broadcasting Service proved to be no different in its view from the other networks. On the one hand this is understandable, since public broadcasting is even more dependent on the government than are the commercial networks and is not in as good a position to defend itself against government influences.

On the other hand, part of PBS's charter is that it should make up for the deficiencies in commercial broadcasting, as to both news and general broadcasting. Yet in its brief, public broadcasting expressed complete approval of what had been said by the commercial broadcasters and the FCC. The summary of its case was as follows:

"The Public Broadcasting Service believes that the issues raised by this petition for review are fully and adequately analyzed in the brief filed by the Commission and that the briefs of the other intervenors will treat those issues as well [this is a kind of approval in advance of the networks' briefs]. PBS believes, therefore, that the lack of merit in McCarthy's legal position is fully demonstrated and that no purpose will be served by the submission of an additional brief making the same points and urging the same positions. Accordingly, pursuant to Rule 28(i) of the Federal Rules of Appellate Procedure, the Public Broadcasting Service herewith adopts the arguments contained in the brief of the Commission. . . ."

There was no need for PBS or the commercial networks to file the same arguments the commission had given in support of its rulings. As a matter of fact, they could have all saved themselves the legal cost and trouble by filing short statements praising the wisdom of the FCC.

Our motion for injunction pending review by the court of appeals was assigned to Judges Carl McGowan and George MacKinnon. They ruled against us, although Judge MacKinnon's concurring opinion supported all of our basic positions. It was another case of a good opinion accompanying a bad decision.

UNITED STATES COURT OF APPEALS
FOR THE DISTRICT OF COLUMBIA CIRCUIT

No. 76-1915   Page 2   September Term, 1976

MacKinnon, *Circuit Judge:* I concur in the judgment that the law does not permit this court, on the record before us, and under the present statute, to order additional participants into the debates between the candidates for the presidency of the two major parties.

As the opinion of the FCC states, the critical factor in "determining whether a debate comes within the section 315(a)(4) exemption is the role and the intent of the broadcaster in covering it" (FCC opinion at p. 8). That is a proper interpretation of the statute, but that is not to say that the complaint of the petitioners is not without considerable merit. To point out the situation the candidates are in, one need only examine the contention of the Columbia Broadcasting System (CBS) before the FCC in this case. CBS asserts that

> A broadcaster is *only* required to make reasonable judgments in good faith *as to the significance of a particular candidate* and so decide how much time should be devoted to coverage of his campaign activities.

Thus, the broadcasters start out by determining how significant a particular *candidate* is. If they determine that *he* is not significant, then the amount of publicity he receives is greatly reduced—he may be effectively "frozen out" from any substantial news coverage during the entire campaign.

If the media had followed a different course and considered that the *candidate* was significant and if the media had given his campaign the same amount of coverage as it did to other candidates, his candidacy might have become of greater "significance" and the candidate might have gone on to win, or to become a serious contender.

But under present practices, as outlined by CBS, a candidate is doomed at the very beginning to having his *personal significance* as a candidate judged by the broadcasters practically before he ever starts his campaign. Thereafter the coverage of the *issues* he raises is correspondingly greatly reduced, and as a candidate he is effectively frozen out of the political campaign by the media. While the present candidates, who are appellants in this proceeding, may by general estimates be far removed from having any reasonable chance to win, the media can just as effectively, behind the screen of "news judgment," by exercising their claimed evaluation of a candidate's personal "significance," reduce its coverage of candidates who might have a chance to win, given fair coverage. And for CBS to argue that the petitioners have not "submitted any specific information to show that CBS's news judgments are unreasonable," merely compounds the error. Candidates that the media freezes out from the beginning will practically never be able to demonstrate that the media's news judgments are unreasonable because they can *never* show how significant their campaign might have become if they had received fair coverage from the beginning for the issues they raised. Thus, the media's early "evaluation" becomes a self-fulfilling prophecy.

The present campaign is a case in point. I venture to suggest that no person would contradict the statement that if one of the appellants received half as much coverage as the candidates of the two principal parties that his vote would be greatly increased.

However, present laws, in my opinion compel us to take the action we have taken today, and only Congress can change it.

Just before the last debate, an appeals court panel affirmed the FCC's decision. The Supreme Court declined to review the case.

A bureaucratic decision, that of the FCC in the Aspen case, had not only denied us access to the people, but canceled out nearly twenty years of legislative history. Commission rulings and court decisions effectively limited political communications by radio and television to what the Republicans and Democrats wish to say.

Bureaucracy:
The Tyranny of the Majority
over the Majority

Alexis de Tocqueville, in his book *Democracy in America*,
wrote of his concern over the inherent danger in democracy
of the "tyranny of the majority." The men who drafted the
Constitution of the United States had also been worried
about such a tyranny and attempted to protect the country
against it. They provided that certain government actions,
such as the ratification of treaties, could not be taken without a two-thirds vote of the Senate, and that amendments
to the Constitution would require the support of more than
a majority of the officials or governmental units involved.
Neither Tocqueville nor the Founding Fathers anticipated
the growth of the bureaucracies and their potential for dom-
inating government.

One hundred years after Tocqueville, historians, political philosophers, and political scientists began to observe, analyze, understand, and explain the operation and
the force of the bureaucracy. The sociologists also became
involved. Some of them described a form of bureaucracy
called "patrimonial," in which the administrative staff is
personally dependent on the head of the system. This is
actually an impure form of bureaucracy—it is better described as an agency. The sociologists identified a second
form of bureaucracy as one subject to "legal domination,"
i.e., its members respond to and carry out a "law" rather
than an executive order.

Hannah Arendt, in her book *The Origins of Totalitarianism*, in which her central interest and concern was totalitarianism of the kind historically manifest in nazism and fascism, made observations that can be applied in the analysis and understanding of bureaucracy operating in other historical circumstances. "Legally," she wrote, "government by bureaucracy is government by decree, and this means that power, which in constitutional government only enforces the law, becomes the direct source of all legislation. Decrees, moreover, remain anonymous (while laws can always be traced to specific men or assemblies), and therefore seem to flow from some overall ruling power that needs no justification." She continued, "There are no general principles which simple reason can understand behind the decree, but ever-changing circumstances which only an expert can know in detail."

"Government by bureaucracy has to be distinguished," she observed, "from the mere outgrowth and deformation of civil services which frequently accompanied the decline of the nation-state." This kind of "civil service," which Arendt associated with the French government, she saw as relatively harmless and inefficient, marked by its capacity to survive all changes and regimes and entrench itself "like a parasite in the body politic" which develops its own interests and becomes "a useless organism whose only purpose appears to be chicanery and prevention of normal economic and political development."

The French, Ms. Arendt observed, "have made the very serious mistake of accepting their administration [that of the inefficient civil service] as a necessary evil," but "they have never committed the fatal error of allowing it to rule the country—even though," she added, "the consequence has been that nobody rules it."

This kind of civil service she saw not as the only alternative to dangerous bureaucracy, but as preferable to the purer bureaucracy in which decrees appeared "in their naked purity, as though they were no longer issued by powerful men, but were the incarnation of power itself and the administrator only its accidental agent."

Ms. Arendt makes two additional points, which although made with reference to the absolutist bureaucracy apply also to bureaucracies and bureaucratic development in non-totalitarian societies. The first is that there are superficial similarities between types of bureaucracies, even between two she describes as marking the outer range of bureaucracy, "especially," she says, "if one pays too much attention to the striking psychological similarity of petty officials."

The second point made by Ms. Arendt was that in Germany and other central European countries, "the state was by definition above the parties," and party leaders as a rule surrendered their party allegiance the moment they became ministers and were charged with official duties. "Disloyalty to one's own party was the duty of everyone in public office," she noted. This conception of government service predated the rise to power of nazism and appears to have made it easier for persons not members of that party to accept and carry out public duties under the Nazi regime.

Both the sociologists' and Arendt's observations apply to bureaucracy in American government. Two agencies of the government now undergoing change resemble the "patrimonial bureaucracy" of the sociologists. These are the FBI and the CIA.

The FBI was a projection of its head, J. Edgar Hoover, whose personal influence affected the methods and operations of the bureau as well as the character of its personnel. Hoover gave the bureau an independence of such strength that a series of Presidents of the United States were either unable or unwilling to challenge the autonomy of its operation.

Without the force of Hoover's personality, it is quite possible that the Federal Bureau of Investigation might have developed into the second form of pure and impersonal bureaucracy and still operated the same way that it did under Hoover. Now that Hoover is gone, the FBI, free of personal authority, may become a greater threat to liberty than it was under J. Edgar Hoover.

The Central Intelligence Agency was not conceived as a "patrimonial" agency in quite the same way as the FBI had been. It was intended to be more of a service agency. In the Eisenhower administration, when Allen Dulles was director and John Foster Dulles was the secretary of state, "patrimonial" power and authority were transferred to the director. It became convenient to assign to the agency responsibility for carrying on activities which, had they been conducted according to traditional State Department or Defense Department methods, would have been subject to congressional scrutiny and in many cases to continuing public judgment, both national and international. Therefore, in some cases their activities would have been clearly seen as violating international law.

Passing such programs on to the CIA and accepting that the agency was justified in using methods of a special order not only removed the programs from challenge, but permitted the use of "more efficient methods." The CIA's apparent success under Eisenhower moved subsequent Presidents to continue to use it as the Eisenhower administration had done.

Since 1952 the agency has been credited with achievements such as these:

• helping oust a premier of Iran in 1953
• helping overthrow a president of Guatemala in 1954
• supporting U-2 intelligence flights over Russia
• sponsoring the Bay of Pigs invasion of Cuba in 1961

- directing a mercenary army in Laos in the 1960s and early 1970s
- playing a prominent role in pacification and other activities in the Vietnam War
- engaging in destabilization activities which encouraged the overthrow of a president of Chile in 1973
- plotting to assassinate "incompatible" world leaders such as Fidel Castro
- and most recently, spying in the United States.

Most of these actions, as well as others for which the agency has been criticized, were carried out with executive approval, if not under its direct order.

The bureaucratic character of the CIA eventually developed to the point at which it could set its course without outside direction. It became an agency that could proceed like the knights who murdered Thomas à Becket, knowing that the act would please the King.

This dynamism of the CIA was essentially that described by C. S. Lewis in an essay called "The Inner Ring." Lewis defined the "Inner Ring" as a group whose members are exempt from rules that apply to other persons or institutions. Its members have a special sense of belonging. The temptation of the "Inner Ring," Lewis says, is strong. It can, he notes, make "a man who is not yet a very bad man do very bad things."

When this strong human drive is given an official function in the service of the republic, it can become even more powerful.

The inner ring of the CIA, or of any intelligence agency, is privileged. Individual responsibility is limited by the oath of loyalty to the agency. Individual conscience is eased in the belief that the agency's goals are good and its untraditional methods accepted. The anonymity of the service, the rejection of name, reward, public recognition, are acts of sacrifice. Doing the wrong things for the right reasons becomes easier until the operation can become an end in itself.

Service in the CIA might be described as a form of secular monasticism. Its membership under Allen Dulles was a highly selective one, drawn from a different cultural background than were members of the FBI, for example, or the Secret Service.

The CIA, however, remained an agency in which personal lines of responsibility could be fixed either on its director or beyond, on the President of the United States, as happened when President Nixon attempted to use it for domestic political purposes as a part of Watergate. The CIA never became a "pure bureaucracy," deriving its strength from "legal domination," or "the incarnation of power itself," the form of pure bureaucracy defined by Hannah Arendt.

Both the FBI and the CIA are inherently management bureaucracies. Possibly they should be termed "agencies," since the FBI is subject to the control of the Justice Department and the CIA is under the President's control.

The Defense Department does not qualify as a bureaucracy, being too large and too complicated. It is rather a separate political society within the larger one of the republic and has, along with its military operations, its own intelligence services, its own participants in foreign policy determination, its own medical services and general welfare programs, including retirement and disability benefits. It has its own retail distribution system in the PX, its own educational system, religious facilities, and ministers. (It was once proposed that a consolidated GI religion be formulated, to serve all members of the armed services and eliminate the need for duplicating or triplicating services, facilities, and clergymen.) It has its own golf courses, its own recreation and rest areas, and as was recently publicized, its own veterinarian service to, among other things, look after the pets of military personnel.

According to a report in 1979, the Defense Department was planning to spend an estimated $57 million to pay the salaries of 667 army and air force veterinarians and their 2,000 assistants. The other military services do not have a veterinary corps, but are entitled to use army and air force services when they need them. A spokesman for the Defense Department defended the service and the expenditure on these grounds:

1. Pets provide a stabilizing influence on the military.
2. Military veterinarians are empowered to treat and prevent diseases in pets that can be contracted by humans. Keeping pets, therefore, protects the health of the military personnel and their families.
3. Veterinarians inspect commissary food and packaged combat rations (something the combat GI will readily believe).
4. Veterinarians care for 2,000 government-owned horses and guard dogs.

Obviously the Defense Department cannot be treated as just another bureaucracy. It has bureaucracies within it. It is, in a way, comparable to the old dirigible hangar at Lakehurst, New Jersey, which was so large that it developed its own weather. When the sun was shining outside, it was possible to have rain inside the hangar, and when the outside weather was calm, it was possible to have wind currents inside.

There are bureaucracies in the structure of the federal government that come much closer to being bureaucracy in its purer form, deriving power from "legal domination" and eventually from "power itself." These receive less attention because their actions are more generalized, less dramatic, less personal, than those of the FBI and the CIA.

Moreover, they resemble the less dangerous agencies of government. The personnel are under civil-service control in regard to pay scales, promotion schedules, special benefits, retirement programs, and so forth. Their political rights are limited by the Hatch Act. Concern over such bureaus and agencies has been largely concentrated on their "efficiency" rather than their internal dynamism and operations.

When I came into the House of Representatives in the 81st Congress, in January 1949, I was advised by John Carson, an old-time political activist from the cooperative movement, not to seek membership on the committees identified by the press and by most members of Congress as powerful or prestigious or both. Rather than asking for committees such as Foreign Affairs, Ways and Means, or Armed Services, he urged me to concentrate on government operations. Carson was a wise man, a longtime observer of government operations both in the United States and in the European parliamentary systems. He saw the government operations committees of the House and the Senate as being in a position to monitor, and even to direct and control, the agencies and bureaucracies of the government. On the other hand, he thought major policy decisions in foreign affairs, taxes, civil rights were determined largely by forces outside the Congress and merely given form by such congressional committees as Ways and Means in the House of Representatives and Finance, Foreign Relations, and Judiciary in the Senate.

When I finally honored Carson's advice (two years before leaving the Senate), I was generally criticized by the press and by other politicians for leaving an "important" committee, Foreign Relations, for a "housekeeping" committee, Government Operations. In twenty years I had learned John Carson's lesson; the press had not.

There is a middle range of bureaucracies, falling between the "patrimonial" and the "legal domination" types, which perform necessary governmental functions reasonably defined by laws, and it includes such agencies, offices, and commissions as the Securities and Exchange Commission, the Federal Trade Commission, the Interstate Commerce Commission, the Civil Aeronautics Board, the Food and Drug Administration, and some, such as the Environmental Protection Agency and the Occupational Safety and Health Administration, of somewhat uncertain jurisdiction.

It is the general responsibility of these institutions to explain, interpret, apply, and, when necessary, enforce the law. Challenging their actions is the principal work of great numbers of lobbyists and lawyers, both in Washington, D.C., and outside the capital city. Their rulings, those that appear to be ridiculous or contradictory, provide an endless supply of material for columnists and cartoonists.

Much of the difficulty with these agencies lies in their responsibility for laws and regulations that attempt to deal with the complexities of American economics, politics, and general culture. Under political pressures, the Congress, supported by the President, often chooses the easy way of passing a law that may be little more than a statement of purpose. Such a law will leave unclear many areas which the agencies of government are expected to clarify, interpret, and define, with the ultimate determination, in too many cases, left to the courts. The "Great Society" program of the Johnson administration, for example, stimulated the establishment of a number of programs that caused bureaucratic difficulties. The general thrust of that program was to make ignorance, mental retardation, ill health, and even ugliness illegal. With such objectives, any government employee or agency charged with the execution of the laws was bound to come up short. Failure and inadequacy of performance has not discouraged the Congress from proposing new and even more far-reaching programs.

There are two reasons for this continuing trend. The first is essentially political: with the breakdown of party discipline and the absence of overriding issues, such as civil rights, members of Congress as well as administrations are looking for issues that are not only attractive to their constituencies but also, if carried out in programs, good.

The second reason for the irresponsible legislative actions is procedural, resulting from reorganizations of Congress. The number of subcommittees has proliferated until there are roughly 250, each with a chairman and a staff. In the House of Representatives, where reform has gone further than it has in the Senate, the seniority system has been effectively challenged, and consequently the power of the committee chairman has been weakened. The discipline of the House Rules Committee, which formerly laid down strict rules for debate and for amending bills before the House of Representatives, has been weakened. In consequence, many more amendments are offered and accepted during floor consideration. The hard line that held that when the House and the Senate were in conference, the views of the House on revenue-raising bills and on appropriations should be highly favored, has been relaxed significantly.

Concerning these changes, Richard Bolling, chairman of the House Rules Committee, has observed that the existence of numerous subcommittees has "increased the opportunity for unskillful people—staff aides and members—to pass bills." And Norman Ornstein, formerly a congressional employee and now a professor of political science, has commented on the freer attitude toward approving amendments during floor debate and has said that while the practice "makes Congress more open, it encourages sloppiness in legislating, because you can't be as careful on the floor as in committee. You can't take 435 people and have them put together a fragile, complex piece of legislation." He predicts pessimistically: "It's likely that bad laws will become even more prevalent in the years ahead." If they do, the power and the responsibility of the civil servants will grow and the involvement of the courts in defining the law will necessarily increase.

Politicians under pressure are driven to seek out issues that are more and more specific in their application. An example of such legislation was a consumer protection bill known as the Magnuson-Moss Warranty Act, signed into law in 1975. Its purpose was to give greater protection to the purchasers of automobiles and appliances. The law did not compel a manufacturer to offer a warranty on its products, but it did provide that if a company offered a "full warranty" it would be required to repair any defect that showed up within a reasonable period of time and to make the replacement or perform the repair work without charge.

As a result, many companies discontinued their "full warranty" policies and replaced them with "limited warranty" guarantees. Some stopped offering warranties altogether. The effect of the law was to give consumers less protection than they had had previously.

In another case, in 1973, Congress directed the Department of Health, Education and Welfare to ban discrimination against the handicapped. The language of the bill was that federal funds must be withheld from institutions that discriminate against an "otherwise qualified handicapped" person. The unanswered question for the bureaucrats at the Department of Health, Education and Welfare was

"Who is handicapped?" Did the phrase include alcoholics or drug addicts as well as the deaf, the blind, and other physically handicapped persons?

A concern over the delay in trial proceedings led Congress to pass the Speedy Trial Act of 1974. The law set a series of deadlines for arraignment and trial following indictment. The rule seemed to be "ready or not, you shall be tried." Now defense lawyers say that they do not have enough time to prepare adequate defenses in many cases. Prosecutors say that the set deadlines force them to delay arrests and ignore some criminals who would otherwise be prosecuted. Judges say that the law is overworking them in the criminal cases, leaving them little time to take up civil cases.

This trend toward sloppy and excessive lawmaking runs contrary to what Alexander Hamilton foresaw for the federal government of the United States. In the *Federalist* No. 17, Hamilton undertook to answer the charge that under the proposed Constitution, the federal government might become so powerful that it would absorb "those residuary authorities, which it might be judged proper to leave with the States for local purposes."

"Allowing the utmost latitude to the love of power which any reasonable man can require," Hamilton wrote, "I confess I am at a loss to discover what temptation the persons intrusted with the administration of the general government could ever feel to divest the States of the authorities of that description. The regulation of the mere domestic police of a State appears to me to hold out slender allurements to ambition." He then listed some of the matters which he thought would never be "desirable cares of a general jurisdiction." Among them he included private justice among citizens of the same state, supervision of agriculture, local needs. And he concluded, "It is therefore improbable that there should exist a disposition in the federal councils to usurp the powers with which they are connected: because the attempt to exercise those powers would be as troublesome as it would be nugatory; and the possession of them, for that reason, would contribute nothing to the dignity, to the importance, or to the splendor of the national government."

When vague and open-ended responsibilities and powers are given over to a bureaucracy, what is likely to follow is beyond prediction. The fault is not always with the bureaucrat, who is (by virtue of the statutes in many cases, and also by the very nature of his function) a person of limited freedom of decision and limited discretionary power. As a result of these limitations he is often in a position in which he can make no decision, and at other times he is in a position when he is compelled to make only such decisions as will be accepted by those who are directing him. The pressure, therefore, on persons making low-level decisions is to err on the side of harsh interpretations and applications of the law, rather than on the side of leniency, and bureaucrats at a higher level follow suit, until an appeal is made to the courts.

The operations of the Environmental Protection Agency demonstrate many of the problems of a bureaucracy charged with administering a body of laws, many of which were drafted in haste and under pressure and with the knowledge on the part of the legislators that administration would be difficult and that controversies over the application of the laws would certainly lead to court cases.

In an article in the *Washington Post* of Sunday, May 20, 1979, John Quarles, formerly deputy administrator of the Environmental Protection Agency, described the growth of that regulatory agency and some of the problems of administering it. Quarles said that recently passed environmental protection laws are defective in two ways: first, in their vagueness and comprehensiveness, and second, in that, as a rule, they set unreasonable timetables for the accomplishment of the purpose of the laws.

The EPA, for example, was given the responsibility to enforce transportation-control programs. Included in the total responsibility were complicated programs to reduce auto pollution, including such things as limiting urban parking, shifting travelers to public transportation, establishing programs for semiannual inspection of automobiles, fitting older cars with pollution-control devices, and almost magically changing the transportation patterns and systems in metropolitan areas. The Congress, advised of difficulties with the administration of the law in 1973, did not get around to changing it until 1977.

Similarly, the 1972 Clean Water Act set an unreasonable schedule for the achievement of its purpose. The law provided that every municipality install secondary treatment plants and meet certain water-quality standards set by July 1977—a provision of questionable constitutional standing in the first place, but also, as experience demonstrated, one beyond physical possibilities of achievement, because of limited funds and shortage of water-purification contractors and equipment.

Quarles cited, as another example of a law that sets an unreasonable deadline, the Resource, Conservation and Recovery Act—an act passed in 1976 to control and direct the disposal of hazardous wastes. It required that a permit program for new plants that produced hazardous waste as a by-product of their operations be in effect within six months after the regulations were promulgated, something which regulatory experts said was in no way possible. The Congress and the President, however, said it must be done.

Another piece of legislation, known as the Delaney Amendment, directed the Food and Drug Administration to ban any food product, and to ban any additive or food-processing chemical from human food, if it has been demonstrated that the substance under question has caused cancer in animals. These requirements moved one administrator to say that the only hope for food processing and medicine rested in developing more cancer-resistant mice. The continuing controversy over the banning of saccharin arose from the attempted application of this law.

The Endangered Species Act similarly has led to difficult bureaucratic decisions, such as those concerning the snail darter and the plant popularly known as the lousewort. A bureaucrat defending the lousewort (threatened with extinction if a dam were built in Maine) argued that the plant might have the secret of birth control and/or prevention of cancer—in other words, the power to prevent life and/or to prevent or at least delay death. These would indeed be considerable powers to find in one plant. The bureaucrat was right, however, in his interpretation of the law, even though there was little likelihood that the plant had the powers he suggested.

Often words in a statute, even though unexplained in reports on the legislation, can, when read by the courts, impose additional responsibilities on government agencies. An example is a case in 1973 in which the Supreme Court directed the Environmental Protection Agency to set up a new program restricting the construction of industrial plants that might cause significant deterioration of air quality in clean-air areas, even though the degree of pollution resulting from the operation of the new plants would be below the level tolerated from plants already in operation in other areas.

This decision was based on three words in the preamble of the Clean Air Act. Preambles of many bills contain declarations of principles that go far beyond anything in the preamble to the Constitution of the United States. A composite of preambles drawn from legislation passed over the past twenty years would certainly cover everything: universal peace, health and happiness for all, life without death, and lions lying down with lambs.

The way a program can escalate is well demonstrated by the growth of the bilingual education program. Involved in its growth were the Congress, the bureaucracy, and the courts. The program began in a limited way as part of the 1968 amendment to the Elementary and Secondary Education Act of 1965. The amendment provided for pilot projects for poor children who were "educationally disadvantaged because of their inability to speak English." One of the sponsors of the program, Senator Alan Cranston of California, noted that it was accepted without any public challenge whatever. What that proves is not clear. Quite possibly the public did not know what was taking place. Possibly the public could not, on short notice, figure out who were the poor children who were "educationally disadvantaged because of their inability to speak English." In any case, the pilot project was to cost $7.5 million.

In 1974, the Supreme Court decided a case brought by Legal Services attorneys in San Francisco on behalf of 1,800 Chinese-speaking students. The attorneys said that the students had been denied special instruction in English. The Supreme Court, accepting that the San Francisco schools were in violation of a 1970 memorandum issued by the HEW Office for Civil Rights—a memorandum based on the 1964 Civil Rights Act which provided that recipients of federal funds cannot be discriminated against on the basis of national origin—ruled that federally funded schools must "rectify the language deficiency" in order to open instruction to students who had "linguistic deficiencies."

Following the Supreme Court decision, HEW threatened other schools with cutoffs unless they recognized the language deficiencies of particular groups. The National Council on Bilingual Education noted that "Cubans admitted after Castro, and more recently, Vietnamese refugees . . . became citizens unintentionally." The Office for Civil Rights in the Department of Health, Education and Welfare targeted 334 schools districts which would have to start "bilingual-bicultural" classes or possibly have their federal funds cut off.

In 1974, the bilingual program was expanded by Congress to include not only poor children but all "limited English-speakers." A new factor was added in the form of a "bicultural education" requirement, that is, an education given with "appreciation for the cultural heritage of such children."

Congressional appropriations for the program increased to $85 million for fiscal year 1975. The Office for Civil Rights estimated that there were 3.6 million "victimized" children of limited English-speaking ability in this country. Congress now contemplates the extension of the program to those of "limited English proficiency in understanding, speaking, reading, and writing." As Tom Bethell noted in a *Harper's* article, this "could be construed as applying to almost anyone in elementary or high school these days."

Meanwhile, the appropriations for 1980 are projected to be $250 million and then to increase by $50 million a year to $400 million in 1983.

The most recent development in the case for being taught the language one speaks, and for being taught in that language, is the demand that Americans who speak a special ethnic or regional kind of English be taught in the language they know and use best.

Above and beyond all other bureaucracies in the federal government there is the Internal Revenue Service. One cannot quite say, as Hitler did of the German state, nothing above the state, nothing against the state, nothing outside the state; but it is close to the truth to say that there is not much in American life that involves the spending, earning, saving, or investing of money that is outside or beyond the interest and the power of the Internal Revenue Service. Of all the agencies, bureaus, offices, and departments of the federal government, the IRS comes closest to being the purest, most nearly perfect bureaucracy. It is detached from personal authority; in most of its operations, it is beyond clear statutory limitations; it is free, if not under pressure, to push its own power to the limits of constitutionality and beyond. It operates on its own dynamism, drawing power from itself, from the concepts of ownership and property use, and from vaguely worded statutes that attempt, in oversimplified language, to deal with complex economic and social institutions, multinationals, corporations, marriages, divorces, religions, racehorses, brood cows, capital gains (both long- and short-term), intentions, assumptions, and more.

The property concept that has gradually been built into the application and the administration of income-tax laws is that no personal or corporate income is, in fact, owned— that it does not become the property of the person or institution that earned it in the year in which it is earned. What is allowed to the earner as his property is that sum which is left after the final tax payment for the earning year. Until that date, the earnings are in the public domain, subject to regulation, to direction, to redistribution.

The original income-tax law (the first one adopted after the passage of the Sixteenth Amendment) was a simple and direct tax, conceived in order to meet the expense of government. The only novel concept in that law was the progressive rate, whereby persons in a higher income bracket were taxed at a higher rate. The law did not undertake any positive social reforms, either by encouraging good works or by discouraging works considered not in the public interest. Such changes were to come later, reflecting, as they were added, not only changing concepts of what was in the public good but also a growing acceptance that the income-tax laws were the principal instrument through which the good society might be achieved.

The Bureau of Internal Revenue began to grow and take on a distinctive bureaucratic character after the passage of the income-tax law in 1913, which imposed a tax on the net income of both individuals and corporations.

The next major changes in the income-tax laws were those included in the Revenue Act of 1918. The act increased earlier income taxes and imposed a normal and surtax rate that went as high as 77 percent of taxable income. The 1918 tax law moved into the area of selective special tax concessions, in that it provided an income-tax credit for individuals and for domestic corporations having foreign income on which income taxes were paid to foreign governments. It also provided liberalized depletion allowances and a punitive tax, later declared unconstitutional, on industries that employed child labor.

In 1919, because of complaints alleging tax fraud and dishonesty among the employees of the bureau in the operation of the Prohibition Unit, six Post Office inspectors were transferred to the Bureau of Internal Revenue, to form the nucleus of the Intelligence Unit. Until 1930, when the Justice Department took over the enforcement of the Volstead Act, primary responsibility for the enforcement of that act had rested with the Prohibition Unit of the Bureau of Internal Revenue.

Dissatisfaction with the administration of the tax laws and the enforcement procedures resulted in the creation of the Board of Tax Appeals in 1924. This board was independent of both the Bureau of Internal Revenue and the Treasury Department.

Another sign of the maturation of the Bureau of Internal Revenue as a bureaucracy was the move to construct a new building, to bring together the employees, previously scattered in a number of locations, into or near the capital city.

The depression years, and the adoption of the Keynesian theory of countercyclical spending by the government, resulted in the passage of tax laws that greatly increased government revenue by raising rates, lowering exemption levels, doubling estate taxes, and imposing gift taxes.

With the passage of the Social Security Act in 1935, administration of the employment taxes required that that law become an additional responsibility of the Bureau of Internal Revenue.

The number of employees continued to grow, increasing from 11,660 in 1933 to 24,046 in 1939, while collections rose from $1.6 to $5.2 billion.

World War II, and the Revenue Act of 1942, marked the shift of the income tax affecting relatively few taxpayers to one affecting great numbers. The increase was accomplished principally by lowering the exemption to $100 for a single person and beginning the surtax at the first dollar of taxable income.

Along with broadening of the base, new methods of collection were devised; withholding taxes from salaries and wages was adopted in 1943. Quarterly payments of estimated taxes were also provided in legislation adopted in 1943.

Microfilming of records was introduced in the forties. The Bureau of Internal Revenue was reorganized in 1952, and its name was changed to the Internal Revenue Service in 1953. To reassure taxpayers that the law was being fairly applied, it expanded its auditing program to include many groups not previously examined.

In 1961, a massive computer center was put into operation in Martinsburg, West Virginia, and in 1966 another center was opened in Detroit. In 1973, the Integrated Data Retrieval System was installed in all Internal Revenue Service regions.

Another computer process, known as the Discriminant Function, was introduced. This process cross-checks as many as fifteen to twenty items on a return, assigning numerical weights to reach its score. Returns with high Discriminant Function scores are turned over to examiners for human judgment as to whether they should be audited or not.

The IRS has added a taxpayers' assistance service. The IRS does not guarantee or stand behind the accuracy of the advice that its personnel give to taxpayers in the preparation of their tax returns, however.

In the sixties, the IRS created a staff to collect information on the financial affairs of right- and left-wing organizations. This unit was first known as the Activist Organization Committee, then as the Special Service Staff (SSS). The SSS was disbanded by order of the commissioner of Internal Revenue in 1973.

A congressional committee later reported that apparently the SSS group was created in response to pressure from the White House and from Congress. The report found that the organizations and individuals were not selected because of possible tax liability or because of the possibility that they might not warrant tax-exemption status, but because of information about their activities revealed in newspapers or in Federal Bureau of Investigation reports. Even though the report found no evidence of clear involvement of senior agency personnel in the activities of the SSS, it did find that the files developed by the special branch were known to higher officers in the service and were being used by them, or at least examined by them.

The IRS had, by the seventies, acquired all of the necessary powers and attributes of a near-perfect bureaucracy. It had its own imperative, drawn in part from law and in part from general social commitment, supplemented by the approval of higher officers of government, including Presidents. It had powers over nearly every citizen of the country. Its judgments carried legal and moral overtones. It had its own court system and its own intelligence service, using most of the devices allowed to agencies like the FBI and the CIA. It had its own building and by 1977 was, with court approval, carrying on internal spying, known as "consensual monitoring"—the label for the practice of secretly monitoring or taping the conversations of IRS employees.

The IRS now is into family planning. Parents are permitted a tax deduction (a reduction in the base upon which the taxes are paid) for each child or dependent. The definition of dependent changes nearly every time the income tax is modified, as does the amount of deductions allowed. Population planners, in order to discourage population growth, regularly propose that no deductions be allowed for increases in family size above a socially approved number. This proposal has not yet been acted upon.

The IRS has moved into other family relationships in the acceptance of the joint return rule and is going tentatively into a more thorough and intimate regulation of income distribution and taxation in cases of divorce, separation, and living-together arrangements.

Tax considerations can determine whether people marry, remain married, or get divorced, and where they live and with whom.

In a recent case involving residents of Puerto Rico, who normally do not pay U.S. income taxes even though they

are citizens of the United States, a husband who had moved
to New York was divorced by his wife, who remained
in Puerto Rico. The woman held that the $17,000-a-
year alimony she received was not taxable, on the grounds
that the alimony payments should have come from her
husband's Puerto Rico income, which exceeded $17,000
a year. The IRS held that her income actually came from
her husband who was living in New York, and that the
alimony payment was taxable by the United States.

IRS involvement in religion would do credit to the court
of the Inquisition, distinguishing the true religion from
heresy. Regularly it makes rulings such as these: the Tax
Court supported an IRS subpoena of membership lists of
a group claiming tax exemption as a religious organization
known as the "All One Faith in One God State Universal
Life Church." The church held that the subpoena would
infringe upon their freedom-of-association rights. The court
held that if deductions were to be claimed by donors, the
IRS had a right to records. The IRS expressed doubts
as to whether the church was a true religion rather
than a front for carrying on a business venture. In contrast,
the IRS accepted that the People's Temple, run by the
Reverend Jim Jones, did meet IRS standards as a religion
eligible for special tax treatment.

In another recent case, the IRS denied the Zion Coptic
Church, Inc., of Miami Beach, Florida, tax exemption as
a "religious body." The IRS imposed a $2.1-million assess-
ment on the church for taxes, penalties, and interest, and
attached $91,000 in cash which police found in the church
in an earlier raid. The use of marijuana is part of this religion, the church claims. In keeping with this declared belief, the church or some of its members were allegedly
involved in a thirty-three-ton marijuana venture.

The IRS is also into decisions about "true education."
Recently it held that the scholarships granted by the Miss

Georgia Scholarship Fund, Inc., a nonprofit organization that solicits, manages, and disburses scholarship money to contestants in the Miss Georgia Contest, were not tax-exempt. The IRS held that the scholarships were not comparable to scholarships that are tax-exempt because they were in fact "compensation" paid to attract high-quality "contestants."

Of a more serious nature are other IRS rulings directed at denying tax deductions for gifts to private schools on grounds of racial discrimination, as the agency attempts to apply civil-rights laws and court interpretations.

The procedural justification for the IRS's authority is that an organization that operates illegally or in a manner contrary to public policy is not "charitable" and therefore is not entitled to the benefits of federal income-tax exemption.

The IRS procedures are not simple. To determine whether a school is racially discriminatory or has an insignificant number of minority students, and whether it was formed or substantially expanded about the time of desegregation of public schools in the community (known as "reviewable schools"), the IRS proposed guidelines for deciding whether tax exemption should be allowed or denied these schools.

To retain tax exemption, schools would have the burden of showing that they met one of two quantitative tests: either that they did have a "significant" minority enrollment or that they, in good faith, operated on a nondiscriminatory basis (good faith was defined as meeting such standards as scholarships for minorities, percentage of minority students and minority faculty, and so forth). Since the first procedures were criticized on policy, procedural, and technical grounds, the IRS is developing new rules.

Opponents of the extension of IRS authority acknowledge the historically demonstrated truth of John Marshall's judgment in *McCulloch* v. *Maryland* that "the power to tax involves the power to destroy," which can be interpreted today also as "the power to deny tax exemption."

The IRS does not hesitate to rule for the sake of public morality and good public behavior. In a recent ruling, sustained by the courts, the IRS argued that a gambling club which financed the activities of shills (whose function was to keep the tables busy) could not deduct the losses of the shills. Under the Internal Revenue Code, gambling losses are deductible only against gambling winnings, which could not be applied in this case.

Reflecting public trends, the IRS, which in the past has ruled that the cost of a course to break the cigarette habit is not deductible as a health expense, has announced that the agency is reconsidering that ruling.

On the positive side, the tax court recently held that there is a sufficient correlation between the prices of finished and feeder cattle to determine that long positions in finished cattle futures could, under proper circumstances, be a legitimate hedging device for feeder cattle. In another case, the tax court overruled the IRS action against a company engaged in chicken and turkey raising, holding that the IRS could not impose the "accrual accounting method" on the fowl operation, since the tax code allows poultry raisers to use "cash accounting."

One of the happiest hunting grounds for the IRS is that of "fringe benefits." Here the fault is not with the agency, which is trying to enforce the letter or the spirit of the law and is often unable to arrive at any clear definition. Periodically (at least every two years) the issue of fringe benefits is raised in the country. Sometimes the initiative comes from the press. Sometimes it comes from the Congress; sometimes it comes from the executive branch itself, as when President Carter denounced the deductibility of what he termed the "three-martini" lunch.

There is also a proposal for "de minimis" exclusions. Meanwhile the IRS is trying to decide which free lunches or other meals are to be included as income and which are to be charged as taxable, whether standard but not custom-made uniforms are deductible, whether the value of parking privileges should be included in income for tax purposes, and so forth. At the same time the statutory exclusions of other benefits, such as contributions to qualified pension plans, group legal services, educational-assistance programs, and moving expenses, are allowed.

In some cases, the IRS imposes tax bills on waiters and waitresses on the assumption that many have not reported their full income from tips. By examining restaurant slips and bills and assuming a 10 to 15 percent gratuity has been added, the IRS assesses the waiters and waitresses for the differences between their reported income and what they would have reported if the gratuities were included. The IRS evidently believes that it has the right to enforce its "assumptions," a right that is not a principle of constitutional law but may well be an operating principle in a bureaucracy. The burden of proving that one's tips did not run as high as the IRS says they did rests on the accused taxpayer.

The IRS has also been and is still involved in activities only marginally related to tax collection. It has been used by law-enforcement officers and other public officials in fighting organized crime. It has been used against suspected criminals. It has lent itself to political uses and abuse.

A new power likely to come to the IRS is that of administering any "income maintenance" or "negative income tax" program. This could be its most important power, and the most challenging one, for the thrust of the "negative income tax" concept is that all incomes should approach equality and, by projection, that all wealth should be equally distributed. If enacted, the negative income tax will open a whole new field for bureaucratic application through the Internal Revenue Service.

The political response to these bureaucratic realities has been minimal and shows no understanding of the nature of the bureaucracy. Both the House of Representatives and the Senate acted to prevent the Internal Revenue Service from denying tax exemption to those private schools which it determines are not making adequate progress toward racial integration.

On September 7, 1979, the Senate voted to amend the Administrative Procedures Act by directing the courts to stop bowing to the agencies as experts in cases involving challenges to their actions. The amendment challenges the long-accepted presumption that agency rules are valid. If accepted by the House, it would shift to the agency the burden of proving, by a "preponderance of the evidence," that its position is right. Whether or not this amendment will have any effect on the way the courts proceed remains to be seen. Until it is passed by the House, it is no more than advice to the courts, which have shown themselves to be quite unmoved by congressional advice that does not have the effect of law.

The reaction to the amendment in some agencies was reported to be one of dismay.

The Federal Trade Commission has become a special target of congressional action. A House of Representatives committee proposes to cut funds for many of the commission's investigations and for the enforcement of some of its rulings.

The senators are considering legislation that would give the Congress the right to veto FTC rulings, in the manner in which it exercises the right to veto rulings and interpretations of law by the Federal Election Commission. Under the threat of congressional action, the administration has modified rules being enforced by the Occupational Safety and Health Administration. The Congress has also overridden some of the decisions of the Environmental Protection Agency and threatens to override more.

But Congress has not yet attacked the substance of the laws responsible for the growth of bureaucratic government. The most common response has been to blame the bureaucrats and to propose making the government more efficient.

This was a major point of emphasis by President Carter when he was campaigning for the presidency, and he has emphasized it since his election. He and the supporters of efficiency seem not to have stopped to ask whether efficiency in the administration of undesirable, badly conceived programs is wise, or whether, on the contrary, things generally might be better, and in some cases individual liberties be better protected, when government is inefficient.

As part of this drive for greater efficiency and greater effectiveness in government, the President proposed reform of the civil service. Congress supported his reforms. The keystone of that plan was said to be the provision establishing within the civil service a Senior Executive Service, to be made up of top career managers whose assignments, pay, and job tenure would depend not upon the standard, orderly procedures by which persons rise through the various levels of civil-service employment to higher and higher positions, but in annual evaluations of individual performance.

Columnists and other experts said clearly that the first test of the plan would lie in the response of the 8,000 persons who had risen to the top of the civil service under the old order. There were some who held that many of this group, according to the stereotypes of the bureaucrat,

would choose security over risk and new challenge. An
early survey by a Washington publication led to a report
that federal personnel managers' estimates of the prospective number who would sign up ranged from 10 percent
to 90 percent—a range of estimates that would suggest
that the survey results were valueless. Nonetheless, they
were published. In 1979 Alan K. Campbell, chairman of
of the Office of Personnel Management (and described
as the architect of the civil-service reform plan), was
reported happy over the fact that, of the first 4,000 civil
servants eligible to make the choice of higher risk for
higher pay, only 19 had refused. Campbell anticipated
that fewer than 50 of the 8,000 eligibles would refuse
to sign up. The sign-up was seen by some observers
as highly significant, indicating that the top-level civil
servant is not a timid, security-conscious person who pre-
fers the safety of a government job to the competitive
realities of the business and professional world outside.
They projected that within seven years the evidence of
greater efficiency and improved performance among government employees will prove that the Senior Executive
Service is a great idea. Putting off the day of reckoning
for seven years will place that day in the middle of the
first term of the President who succeeds the next elected
President.

Seven is a mystical number, and also a good political
number. It will carry the country beyond a presidential-
election year and the government to a point where who-
ever is President can again propose a reorganization of the
civil-service system in the name of efficiency.

Seven is also a prime number like eleven, thirteen,
seventeen, and so on (that is, it is not divisible by any other
whole number). Prime numbers are important, according
to Lyt Wood, county forester of Rappahannock County,
Virginia, in explaining the survival of thirteen- and seven-

teen-year locusts. According to Lyt, any prime predator would have to have a life span identical with that of the locust. With a seventeen-year life span, Lyt points out, the locusts arrive in such numbers that they overwhelm predators in something described as "predator satiation." The same is true of thirteen-year locusts.

The seven-year postponement of the testing of the new civil-service plan gives the program and those who participate in it a seven-year protection from predatory critics.

It is not surprising that the sign-up among the 8,000 has been so high. Those civil servants who have made it to the top, or near the top, are resourceful and intelligent. They are not unmindful of the ways of the service, or careless about achieving and maintaining their various job ratings in grade and through other promotions. They keep track of such things as sick leave, vacation time, and terminal leave. They know about their government insurance policies and certainly about their pensions and retirement benefits. They are reported to be concerned about their office space, their office furniture, and their preferential parking places.

The benefits of participating in the new program seem obvious: a potential $66,000 a year, rather than $47,500, as well as the possibility of more interesting or at least different work, a better retirement base, and so forth. The risks seem minimal, first because most top-level civil-service persons are competent, or if not, have been able to conceal their incompetence on the way to the top levels of government employment. Second, under the new order of things, they are likely to be performing duties very similar to those they have been performing. Third, for the most part, their performance will be judged by the same persons, or the same kinds of persons, who have been judging it in the past. Fourth, there is little danger of significant political interference. Fifth, demotion will result in the employee's being put back into his original rank. This, advocates of the plan say, will stigmatize the employee. Theoretically, the possibility of carrying that stigma through the rest of one's career should move the incompetent person not to take the risks of the Senior Executive Service, or if one does, to work harder, even to the point of becoming an overachiever.

It has not been suggested that those who fail be required to wear special garb indicating their disgrace, nor is it recommended that they be shunned by their co-workers. The numbers that will be dismissed, or excluded from the car pools, one can safely assume, will be no greater than is the case under existing rules and practices. Moreover, what with the gasoline shortage and the pressure to force government employees to pay for their parking, and with the IRS waiting to rule that parking privileges must be translated into cash value and included in income for tax purposes, even the loss of special, highly desirable parking rights would be easier to bear than it would have been five years ago.

A second procedural approach to the better control of the bureaucracies, at least those that deal with regulations, has been initiated by the Carter administration, with a regulatory council.

The council, set up by the President, is supposed to carry an overview (a continuing one) of the regulatory agencies. It is supposed to set up a list of priorities—that is, a list of things needing immediate regulation, or at least regulation ahead of other things that may need regulation. It is also responsible for preventing duplication and for encouraging coordination among the many regulatory agencies in Washington.

Under challenge and criticism, the White House responded by saying that the council is a "creature of the regulators themselves." This explanation closes the circle for those who could challenge a system in which the regulators are going to regulate themselves.

While making these marginal challenges to federal bureaucracies, the Congress and the President have concurred in establishing a new Department of Education. Federal responsibilities and power over education used to be carried out through the Office of Education, a part of the Department of Health, Education and Welfare.

Opponents of the proposal to set up the department were assured by its proponents that the department would have no authority not already exercised through the Office of Education. It is very doubtful that the new department will be so restrained, and it seems likely that progressively there will be more and more federal control and intervention in the educational institutions and programs of the country. The Office of Education, without cabinet status, has already shown a willingness to intrude into private schools as well as public schools.

On the other hand, the National Endowment for the Arts, operating with a very limited budget, goes to extremes to avoid anything that might be considered interference with the artistic process. Yet it does decide which artistic projects should be supported and is committed to developing an "artistic consciousness." Someone in the Endowment will have to decide what that "artistic consciousness" is to be.

The old rule that "he who pays the fiddler calls the tune" still applies. Maurice Abravanel, music director of the Utah Symphony, in addressing a conference on government and individual liberty sponsored by the Center for the Study of Democratic Institutions, held in Washington, D.C., said that because of government support, the Utah Symphony programs had been changed somewhat and recalled "seeing a National Endowment movie of an old sharecropper singing to his banjo, and one council member saying, 'In its way, that is just as much art as is the singing of Beverly Sills.'

"As a musician," he commented, "I could not agree with him, but as a human being I think he has a point."

Intervention by the Department of Education is most likely to be manifest in three general areas. One is the enforcement of desegregation laws, and seeking greater integration in the nation's schools. Second is the pursuit of the objective of equal educational opportunity, which involves sex, race, ethnic, and language differences, and differences in income and wealth. Third is determining standards and content for schools, with the possibility of governmentally directed testing programs, nationally directed college admission policies, nationally determined standards for academic progress, and a nationally approved curriculum.

With this new department added to the rest, four major areas in which individual liberty should be protected—economic, political, educational, and artistic, symbolized in Irish tradition by the plow, the sword, the book, and the harp—are all laid open to bureaucratic attack, all in the name of equity, of efficiency, and more, in the pursuit of moralistic perfection.

As Gilbert Chesterton said, the puritans continue to carry out their function of killing St. George and saving the dragon. And, as Robert Lowell identified it, the harsh, high laughter of the innocent is heard rejoicing over their victories.

Index

press and, 146–50
state laws protecting, 118–33
strengthening of, 26–29
Supreme Court opinions and, 85–86, 120–21, 124–25, 127

Udall, Morris, 45
United States Chamber of Commerce, 97
Utah, two-party system in, 124

Vanderbilt Law Review, 113, 116
Vermont, two-party system in, 124
Volstead Act, 201
Voting age, and Twenty-sixth Amendment, 12–13
Voting Age Population (VAP), 43

Wallace, George, 118, 120, 121, 147, 166
Wallace, Henry, 118, 166
Warranties, 193
Washington, George, 24

Washington Post, 135, 137, 143, 161, 195
Washington Star, 99
Watergate, 42, 43–44, 53, 54, 188
press and, 138–39
Wertheimer, Fred, 50
What I Saw in America (Chesterton), 6
White, Byron, 57
White, Theodore, 138
Wiley, Richard, 161, 162
Wilkey, Malcolm R., 49
dissent in *Buckley* v. *Valeo,* 71, 73
Williams v. *Rhodes,* 120
Wilson, Woodrow, 16, 33
Winter, Ralph, Jr., 49, 58–61, 76–77
Women's suffrage, and Nineteenth Amendment, 12
Wood, Lyt, 211–12
Woodward, Bob, 138, 139
Wright, Skelly, 49
Write-in voting, 130–32

Zagoria, Sam, 110, 111
Zapple, Nicholas, 161
Zapple case, 155–56